Perfect
PROJECTS

OTHER BOOKS BY JEANNI GOULD:

10 Terrific Programs for New Beginnings and Young Women in Excellence (with Rebekah Lowe)

Midweek Treasures for Young Women

Perfect PROJECTS

for PERSONAL PROGRESS

Includes 43 Value Experiences, 22 Projects, and 7 Original Songs

JEANNI GOULD

Covenant Communications, Inc.

ACKNOWLEDGMENTS

This is the last year all my children will be teenagers.
Thanks for the inspiration. I love you very much.

And to Brian—my love always. You are so close to perfect,
I am continually trying to push you over the edge.

Cover & title page illustrations © Kristine A. Mackessy

Cover design copyrighted 2002 by Covenant Communications, Inc.

Published by Covenant Communications, Inc.
American Fork, Utah

Printed in Canada
First Printing: August 2002

09 08 07 06 05 04 03 02   10 9 8 7 6 5 4 3 2 1

ISBN 1-59156-035-7

Foreword

Truly Personal Progress

Personal Progress Program: Young Women must accomplish 42 short Value Experiences, plus 7 long (10 hours minimum) Value Projects, to earn the Young Women Recognition award. In counsel with leaders and parents, young women may design 14 of the Value Experiences, and all 7 Value Projects, to suit individual interests! Girls can progress at their own rates, so enthusiastic Beehives can sail through half (or all) of their total goals and requirements. With the expanded scope for personal choice, you can truly customize your Personal Progress to help accomplish your goals and dreams.

Help is here! You'll appreciate the wonderful hands-on ideas for the updated Personal Progress Program in this new book by Jeanni Gould! This book contains suggestions for over 43 Value Experiences and 22 Value Projects, with a bonus of 7 new spiritual songs written especially for young women! Ideas range from independent goals to Young Women activities to family home evenings.

Perfect Projects offers a wide variety of suggestions to help young women advance through the Personal Progress Program, and earn the Young Women Recognition award. This book will not only help Young Women leaders encourage the youth, it will also give parents a warm and positive way to work with their teenage daughters!

About Jeanni Gould

This is Jeanni's third book for young women. Her previous books are also available in music CD/CD-ROM form, including performances of all the songs:
- *10 Terrific Programs for New Beginnings and Young Women in Excellence* (co-written with Rebekah Lowe)
- *Midweek Treasures for Young Women*

Jeanni has a degree in English literature and an enduring love of all the arts. An award-winning composer, Jeanni writes frequently for choirs as well as for women's groups and solos. Her "day job" as a mom and music teacher gives her plenty of time to write—at night! In her spare time, she loves to snowboard with her wonderful husband Brian and her two teenage children. Jeanni is honored to have served with the youth for most of her life. Please e-mail Jeanni at info@covenant-lds.com.

Table of Contents

FAITH

DIVINE NATURE

INDIVIDUAL WORTH

KNOWLEDGE

CHOICE AND ACCOUNTABILITY

GOOD WORKS

INTEGRITY

*Choose how you want to accomplish each Value Experience or Project:

**I = individual activity, F = family activity, YW = Young Women activity,
YW/YM = joint Young Women and Young Men activity**

How to Use This Book

Hands-on Help

This book lets you choose from more than 6 different Value Experiences for each Young Women value—over 43 in all! Many can be carried out during the regular Mutual activity, to help and encourage the progress of all participants. This book also offers plans for family involvement, including family home evening ideas, to help young women strengthen their homes and families. In counsel with your leaders and parents, you can use this book to design 14 Value Experiences and 7 Value Projects to help you develop into the woman you want to become.

Perfect Projects!

Oh my! Every girl must plan and carry out 7 different ten-hour Value Projects? This daunting task facing young women, leaders, and parents is made easy with the creative, fun, family and service-oriented projects in this book! Included are 3 or more project ideas for each value—a total of more than 22 projects! You may use the experiences and projects just as they are written in this book. Everything you will need is included: supply lists, time allowances, handouts, invitations, helpful hints, etc. These ideas will spark your own imagination, helping you create the best ever Personal Progress program!

Songs to Bring the Spirit

Can you remember the names of your Primary teachers? No? But you can probably still sing *every song*! Put the incredible power of music to work in a positive way in your life! This book includes 7 meaningful songs that are beautiful and fun to sing. The songs also have a more important purpose: to reinforce righteous principles and to increase your faith in the Lord.

Learning these songs can fulfill Value Experiences in each of the 7 areas. Plus, for an effective Value Project, a young woman can take the lead: teach a song to others, and then arrange a performance. All songs are appropriate for Young Women meetings, sacrament meetings, special musical numbers, family home evenings, activities, firesides, and other special events. Sacred music draws the Spirit near.

FAITH

Faith

VALUE EXPERIENCE

Sing a Joyful Song!

Do you remember the names of any of your Primary teachers? Probably not, but you can most likely remember *every single song*! Put the incredible power of music to work in a positive way in your life. Music, more than anything on earth, helps to bring the Spirit near.

On your own: Study and learn the lyrics of the song "Celebrate!" on pages 18–21 of this book. Play, or ask someone to play the music, as you sing the words. Rejoice in the wondrous creations of the Lord, and express gratitude for His love that lifts and strengthens you each day. You will feel joyful as you celebrate the Lord's goodness in song.

With your family: Learn and sing this song for a special family home evening. Lead a family discussion about the things that bring you joy.

As a Young Women's group: Learn and sing "Celebrate!" in Young Women meetings. The song is very upbeat, quick, and fun to sing!

GOALS: Sing a song of praise to the Lord.

Feel the joy of being part of the eternal plan of happiness.

Commit to more fully express your appreciation to Heavenly Father and the Savior in your prayers this week.

TIME: 30–60 minutes to learn and sing the song several times

HANDOUTS: Music for the song "Celebrate!" on pages 18–21

SUPPLIES: Copies of the music
            Singers divided into two groups
            Piano and pianist

HINT: Do you love to perform? Arrange with your leaders for your Young Women's group to sing this song as a special musical number.

PROJECT: You can expand this activity into a Value Project by directing a Young Women's choir as they prepare and perform this song:

FAITH VALUE PROJECT
Teach a Song: "Celebrate!" p. 16

Faith

VALUE EXPERIENCE
Temple Trip

Remember the peace you feel as you walk around the temple grounds? Share that wonderful experience with a friend! Invite someone you care about to join you in a visit to the nearest temple. Explain that, while you cannot enter the temple itself at this time, there are many things to do in the visitors' center, and there are lovely sights to enjoy while strolling the beautiful gardens surrounding the temple.

Things to do in the visitors' center: Stand reverently before a statue or painting of Christ. Discover scriptures in many different languages. Select from a wide list of short movies to view in the theater.

With your family: Invite a neighbor family to come with you to see the beautiful building, and the lovely gardens on the temple grounds. Warm up (or cool off) inside, as you take a tour of the visitors' center.

For a Young Women or YW/YM activity: Invite all the youth to bring friends to attend a local temple pageant or view the Christmas lights display.

HINT: Ask to see the short video, *Best of Homefront II*, which includes 21 inspiring messages created for television viewers. This video is hilarious and touching.

GOALS: Give your friend an opportunity to feel the presence of the Holy Ghost.

                 Express to your friend your belief that, through covenants made in this temple, families can be together after death.

TIME: 1–2 hours, plus travel time

SUPPLIES: Outdoor clothing appropriate to the weather

BONUS: Extra special times to visit the temple:
Christmas lights display at the temple grounds
Annual outdoor pageant
Open house of a newly constructed temple
Note: obtain free advance tickets at
www.lds.org.

Faith

VALUE EXPERIENCE

Book of Mormon Boost

Develop a pattern of regular scripture reading in your life. Each day for one month, read two pages of the Book of Mormon. Pray sincerely before you begin that you will be blessed to understand God's word.

With your family: Challenge your parents to do this experience with you!

GOALS: Increase your trust in the Lord as you read of His love for His children. (See 1 Nephi 11:17.)

Develop a habit of regular scripture reading. (See Alma 32:28.)

Follow the instructions of the prophets. (See Moroni 10:4.)

TIME: 8–10 minutes per day, one hour per week, four hours total

HANDOUT: Scripture Reading Chart on page 5

SUPPLIES: Book of Mormon
Scripture marking pencil
Copy of Scripture Reading Chart
Marker or stickers to mark chart
Peace and quiet

HINT: Buy cute miniature stickers to show your progress on the chart!

PROJECT: Continue reading two pages daily for the next nine or ten months, and you will finish the entire Book of Mormon!

FAITH VALUE PROJECT
Book of Mormon, p. 12

Book of Mormon Boost
One Month Scripture Reading Chart

	Day 1	Day 2	Day 3	Day 4	Day 5	Day 6	Day 7
Week One							Checkpoint: 1 Nephi 8
Week Two							Checkpoint: 1 Nephi 14
Week Three							Checkpoint: 1 Nephi 18
Week Four							Checkpoint: 2 Nephi 2
Week Five							Checkpoint: 2 Nephi 8

Read two pages each day, and then place a sticker or mark in the space.

Faith

VALUE EXPERIENCE

Bear It Bravely

Bear your testimony in sacrament meeting. Tell of your love for the scriptures that testify of Jesus Christ.

Express your faith that the Lord has atoned for our sins, and that through the plan of salvation we can live with our families, our Savior, and our Heavenly Father again. Testify that our prophet speaks to the Lord and receives direct revelation from the Lord for our lives.

GOALS: Share the joy of knowing Jesus Christ as your example and Savior.

Prepare to stand as a witness of your faith, now and in the future.

JOURNAL: Record your testimony.

TIME: 30 minutes: Gathering your courage
5 minutes: Bearing testimony

HINT: Read and mark Moroni 10:3–5.

PROJECT: To receive the greatest benefit from this experience, first complete the following Value Project:

FAITH VALUE PROJECT
Book of Mormon, p. 12

Faith

VALUE EXPERIENCE

Scripture Sign

Carefully and prayerfully select a scripture verse that is especially meaningful to you. Mark the passage in your scriptures so you will always remember it.

On a large poster board, carefully write out the entire scripture, including the reference. Then decorate the poster with appropriate and inspiring artwork.

Hang this scripture sign on a wall or door in your bedroom. Memorize the scripture and reference, and try to act upon it for the next two weeks.

With your family: You may want to share your scripture and display your poster for family home evening.

For a Young Women activity: Meet as a Young Women's group. Ask every girl to quietly search her scriptures for a verse or short passage that has a particularly important message for her. Allow a few minutes, and then invite each young woman to take a moment to share her selected verse. Each girl then creates and decorates a poster featuring her scripture.

GOALS: As the prophet Nephi counseled, apply the scriptures to yourself. (See 1 Nephi 19:23.)

Create a wholesome and uplifting decoration for your room.

TIME: 30–60 minutes, depending on your artistic inspiration

"My sheep hear my voice, and I know them, and they follow me."
John 10:27

SUPPLIES: Complete set of scriptures
Scripture marking pencil
Ruler or yardstick
Pencil
Markers or paints
Stickers, glitter, etc., to decorate poster
Poster tape that won't damage walls

Faith

VALUE EXPERIENCE

P.R.A.Y.

Enhance your prayers using this simple and sweet acronym: P.R.A.Y. (Praise. Repent. Ask. Yield). Pray sincerely, using this pattern, two times each day for one month. Make your prayers more meaningful as you take time to listen and ponder.

Use the P.R.A.Y. outline on the following page to remind yourself of these four steps of prayer.

GOALS: Communicate more fully with Heavenly Father, gaining a greater appreciation of His plan, His righteousness, and His all-encompassing love for you as his daughter.

Establish an unfailing pattern of thoughtful and earnest prayer.

Practice humble acceptance of the Lord's will.

TIME: Approximately 15 minutes each day

HANDOUT: P.R.A.Y. outline on page 9

SUPPLIES: P.R.A.Y. outline
Peace and quiet

HINT: Read Enos chapters 4–6, and imagine praying, with all your heart, all day long and into the night. Through Enos's sincere prayer, in that one day, his sins were forgiven. It's hard to comprehend the peace and joy such a prayer would bring.

This blessing is available to each of us. Heavenly Father is just waiting for us to ask!

P.R.A.Y.

P   PRAISE: Ponder with sincere appreciation all that Heavenly Father has given you. Express your thankfulness and praise to Him.

R   REPENT: With genuine remorse, ask for forgiveness of your sins, and resolve to choose the right in similar future situations.

A   ASK: Blessings are waiting to shower down on you. All you need to do is humbly request those things you are in need of.

Y   YIELD: This is the most difficult thing to remember. After you have asked for help, stay on your knees, pondering and listening for the answers you need. This quiet time allows Heavenly Father to bless you with knowledge and comfort.

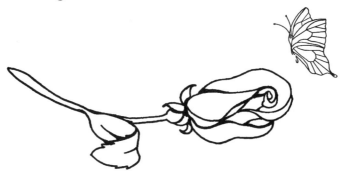

Faith

VALUE EXPERIENCE

Spiritual Survival Kit

Get ready now to meet the personal challenges ahead! Gather items you will find critically important to your spiritual survival, and place them in a small packet to take with you everywhere, every day!

With your family: Work together to prepare a "Spiritual Survival Kit" for each family member. As you place each item into the kit, take turns imagining a potential situation where this spiritual reminder would benefit you.

GOALS: Recognize that you must prepare in advance to avoid falling for the temptations of Satan.

Remind yourself on a regular basis (every time you open your backpack at school) of what is truly important.

TIME: 30 minutes or longer, depending on your inspiration

HANDOUTS: Spiritual Survival Kit List on page 11

SUPPLIES: Copy of Spiritual Survival Kit List
Small reclosable case, or plastic zipper bag
Articles of Faith card
Favorite scripture, written in tiny letters on a card
Band-aid
Stick of gum
Eraser
Safety pin
Quarter
Tootsie roll
Tiny teddy bear or other toy

HINT: Prepare a kit for yourself and several for your friends!

PROJECT: Share your secrets of spiritual health day by day. Plan, prepare, and present a Young Women Mutual activity on this topic. Provide materials and assist each participant in making her own "Spiritual Survival Kit."

10

Spiritual Survival Kit List

Articles of Faith card, ready for you to stand as a witness
Tiny toy, to remind you that you are a child of God
Safety pin, to represent how your family can be together forever
Tootsie roll, to feed your spirit as well as your body
Favorite scripture, your Rx for spiritual health
Quarter, to remember you can always "call home"
Stick of gum, to remember to "chews" the right
Band-aid, for sore knees from much praying
Eraser, to remind you to forgive others

Spiritual Survival Kit List

Articles of Faith card, ready for you to stand as a witness
Tiny toy, to remind you that you are a child of God
Safety pin, to represent how your family can be together forever
Tootsie roll, to feed your spirit as well as your body
Favorite scripture, your Rx for spiritual health
Quarter, to remember you can always "call home"
Stick of gum, to remember to "chews" the right
Band-aid, for sore knees from much praying
Eraser, to remind you to forgive others

Faith

VALUE PROJECT

Book of Mormon

Commit to read the Book of Mormon this year, and to draw nearer to the Savior. By reading two pages (only two!) each day, you will complete the entire Book of Mormon with almost three months to spare! The prophet Ezra Taft Benson counseled us, *"The Book of Mormon brings men to Christ…. It tells in a plain manner of Christ and His gospel. It testifies of His divinity and of the necessity for a Redeemer and the need of our putting trust in Him…. and all other things are secondary. The golden question of the Book of Mormon is 'Do you want to learn more of Christ?'"* (Ensign, Jan. 1988, 3–4).

Complete the Book of Mormon Scripture Reading Chart on page 13 as you progress chapter by chapter, and book by book. This visual reminder of your Value Project will let you see the progress you have made. The chart will also encourage you to reach your final goal.

GOAL: Say with personal knowledge, "I know the Book of Mormon is true."

TIME: Large, but worth it! Between 20 and 40 hours total, depending on how fast you read, and how much you ponder along the way. Slower can be better!

HANDOUT: Book of Mormon Scripture Reading Chart on page 13

SUPPLIES: Book of Mormon
Copy of Book of Mormon Scripture Reading Chart
Scripture marking pencils in cool colors

HINT: Mark scriptures that touch your heart or are especially meaningful to you. As you read the next time, and the time after that, you will appreciate seeing what you enjoyed and learned in the past. You will be able to track your spiritual growth!

BONUS: This is a major goal. Your commitment will pay off, so don't give up! If you are struggling to stick with it, work on this complementary project at the same time:

INTEGRITY VALUE PROJECT
You Should be Committed! p. 128

Book of Mormon
Scripture Reading Chart

BEGIN TO READ	Day 1													
WEEK 3 & 4												Finish 1 Nephi		
WEEK 5 & 6														
WEEK 7 & 8														
WEEK 9 & 10		Finish 2 Nephi										Finish Jacob		Finish Enos
WEEK 11 & 12	Read Jarom	Read Omni	Read Words of Mormon											
WEEK 13 & 14														
WEEK 15 & 16							Finish Mosiah							
WEEK 17 & 18														
WEEK 19 & 20										Halfway Point Alma 23				
WEEK 21 & 22														
WEEK 23 & 24														
WEEK 25 & 26														
WEEK 27 & 28			Finish Alma											
WEEK 29 & 30									Finish Helaman					
WEEK 31 & 32														
WEEK 33 & 34												Finish 3 Nephi		Finish 4 Nephi
WEEK 35 & 36										Finish Mormon				
WEEK 37 & 38												Finish Ether		
WEEK 39 & 40					Finish Moroni	*	CON -	GRAT	- U -	LA -	TIONS	!	*	

Read two pages each day, and then place a sticker or mark in the space.
A completion space for each book is shown, so you can see your progress!

Faith

VALUE PROJECT

The Six B's

President Gordon B. Hinckley challenged the youth of the Church. *"I hope that you are studying diligently and that your great ambition is to get A grades in your various courses…. Tonight I am going to let your teachers give you the A's that I hope you earn. I want to talk about some B's. You get the A's; I will give you the B's.*

> *Be grateful.*
> *Be smart.*
> *Be clean.*
> *Be true.*
> *Be humble.*
> *Be prayerful."*

("A Prophet's Counsel and Prayer for Youth," *Ensign,* Jan. 2001, 2.)

With approval from your Young Women leaders, prepare a display that represent President Hinckley's six B's. Organize objects, quotes, photos, scriptures, handouts, or other items to show how you are making efforts to incorporate each concept into your life.

Invite the young women in your ward to view your display. Give every girl a copy of the Six B's card (on page 15). Ask each young woman to post the card on her bathroom mirror, and then read and think about the prophet's counsel every day.

GOALS: "Be" knowledgeable about President Hinckley's counsel to the youth.

"Be" prepared to explain the importance of each character trait.

"Be" an example for the other young women in your ward.

TIME: 10+ hours

HANDOUT: Decorated card of the Six B's on page 15

SUPPLIES: Large table
Tablecloth
Poster of each of the six B's
Items of your choice to display
Copies of the Six B's card

VALUE EXPERIENCE: Young women may be inspired to work on this:
FAITH VALUE EXPERIENCE
P.R.A.Y., p. 8

Six B's

Be Grateful
Be Smart
Be Clean
Be True
Be Humble
Be Prayerful

Gordon B. Hinckley

Six B's

Be Grateful
Be Smart
Be Clean
Be True
Be Humble
Be Prayerful

Gordon B. Hinckley

Faith

VALUE PROJECT

Teach a Song: "Celebrate!"

"For my soul delighteth in the song of the heart; yea, the song of the righteous is a prayer unto me, and it shall be answered with a blessing upon their heads. Wherefore, lift up thy heart and rejoice." D&C 25:12–13

With approval from your Young Women leaders, learn and then help teach the new song "Celebrate!" to a group of young women. Arrange an opportunity for them to perform as a choir. This is a very upbeat song that will have you tapping your toe and smiling as you sing! That's why it's titled "Celebrate!"

LEARN: Study and learn the lyrics of "Celebrate!" on pages 18–21 of this book. Play, or ask someone to play the music, as you sing the words. Notice that there are two parts: one for sopranos and one for altos. Both parts are very easy to learn and sing. Most of the time everyone sings the melody together. The occasional harmony adds richness and excitement to the song.

TEACH: After you are familiar with the melody and harmony, you can begin to teach it to others. First have everyone learn the melody, "Singing with joy we celebrate, praising the Savior; Singing with joy we celebrate, praising the Lord." Then divide into two groups; the soprano part will be for young women who enjoy singing high, while the alto part will be for young women who can sing lower. The alto part is best for young women who can read music or are experienced at singing harmony.

As you sing together, appreciate the happy upbeat rhythm and the fun sound of the harmony. You will feel joyful as you celebrate the Lord's goodness in song.

PERFORM: Choose a performance date about six weeks ahead, to allow time to polish all parts. Lead the Young Women's group as they sing "Celebrate!" for your ward's sacrament meeting or another special occasion.

GOALS: Sing a joyful song of gratitude for the Lord's goodness.

                Increase leadership skills as you make arrangements, teach, and lead rehearsals and performances.

                Follow through with your commitment, even if others are not always dependable.

Teach a Song:
"Celebrate!"
(CONTINUED)

TIME: 10+ hours, including time to
- Study the lyrics and understand the message of the song
- Sing and play through the song several times
- Arrange with leaders for dates to teach it to young women
- Copy and organize the sheet music
- Learn how to teach and direct music
- Notify and remind choir members of practice times
- Arrange performance date with ward music chair
- Plan, set up space, and lead musical rehearsals
- Warm up and perform

HANDOUTS: Music for the song "Celebrate!" on pages 18–21

SUPPLIES: Copies of the sheet music for all young women choir members
Music folders (optional but gives an elegant look as you perform)
Person who is knowledgeable about music and willing to assist
Singers divided into two groups
Piano and pianist
Name and phone number of ward music chair
Calendar to check dates
Treats (optional but rewarding at the end of song practice)

HINTS: To include all your ward's young women in your choir, ask your Young Women leaders if they will allow you to teach and to practice the music during opening exercises on Sundays. Be sure to schedule in advance which Sundays you may rehearse. Be careful to stick to the time limit they give you.

Suggest to the choir members that they smile as they sing this song. This will show their joy in the Savior's love; plus it will keep them from singing flat!

VALUE EXPERIENCE:
Young Women singers may accomplish a Value Experience as they participate in this group:

FAITH VALUE EXPERIENCE
Sing a Joyful Song! p. 2

Celebrate!

Words & Music by
Jeanni Hepworth Gould

Joyfully, ♩ = 172

Soprano & Alto duet

(Unison) Sing - ing with joy, we cel - e - brate,

prais - ing the Sav - ior; Sing - ing with joy, we cel - e - brate, prais - ing the Lord.

Glo - ry and pow'r and hon - or for all He has giv - en, Lift - ing our voice with grat - i - tude

ris - ing to heav'n. May our hearts share the sto - ry, sing - ing of His glo - ry!

Doctrine & Covenants 25:12-13

19

We will praise the Sav - ior. Cel - e - brate, prais - ing the Lord. For the
Sav - ior. Sing-ing with joy we cel - e - brate, prais-ing the Lord. For the

King of cre - a - tion, shout with ex-ul - ta - tion! Sing-ing with joy, we
King of cre - a - tion, shout and praise the Lord!

cel - e - brate, prais - ing the Lord. All sing
Cel - e - brate, prais - ing the Lord. *Slower*

"Al - le - lu - ia;" Voic - es ring in

20

DIVINE NATURE

Divine Nature

VALUE EXPERIENCE

Birthday Twist

On your own birthday: Celebrate your birthday with an unusual twist. Give a gift to your mother! Explain that you wish to express your appreciation to her for giving you the gift of life. You want very much to thank her for the innumerable gifts she has given you every day since you were born. Treat her with the greatest kindness on this special day.

How to: Start the day by preparing and serving your mother breakfast in bed. She has already "labored" on this date; today she should rest a little! There are other kind acts of service you may wish to offer to your mother today: style her hair, cheerfully run errands, give her a pedicure, watch your younger siblings, etc. You may find that as you show your love to your mother on your birthday, it will become one of the best birthdays you'll ever celebrate!

With your family: Show family members, by your loving example, that you want to celebrate not only your birth, but also the loving goodness of your mother. Your attitude will influence other family members in a positive way.

GOALS: Realize your mother is a beloved daughter of God who has given you a wonderful gift.

               Demonstrate your love and appreciation for the service she offers willingly each day.

TIME: 30–60 minutes to prepare and serve breakfast

SUPPLIES: Flower in small vase
Tray
Food ingredients for breakfast of your choice
Napkin, plate, silverware, glass
Thank-You card

HINT: You may want to try this for an "Un-Birthday Surprise!"

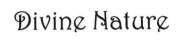

Divine Nature

VALUE EXPERIENCE

Ancestor Evening

With your family: Learn of your ancestor's life and the events that shaped his or her history, as you select and discuss this "family heirloom" with your parents.

For a Young Women activity: Invite young women to come prepared with one special object that belonged to a personal ancestor. Sitting in a large circle, each young woman can show her "family heirloom" and tell a personal story about the ancestor who owned or used that item. The object may be small or large, beautiful or simple, valuable or not, but will cause each young woman to reflect on her family history and make a connection to her eternal roots.

GOALS: Understand the roots and history of your family.

Feel a desire to learn more of your ancestors.

Better appreciate the challenges and accomplishments of your ancestors.

TIME: 30–60 minutes

HANDOUT: Invitation on page 25

SUPPLIES: Invitations
Family "heirlooms" brought by young women
Oral history of each item

HINT: Examples of "family heirlooms" you can share:
      Great-grandmother's handkerchief
      Book in a different language, carried to America by ancestor
      Violin or other antique that's been in the family for generations
      Handmade quilt
      Letters written by your great-grandparents to your grandfather
      on his mission

Please come to an Ancestor Evening!

Date: _____

Time: _____

Place: _____

Please bring a special "heirloom"
that belonged to one of your ancestors.
Be prepared to share a story about
your ancestor and the item you chose.

Please come to an Ancestor Evening!

Date: _____

Time: _____

Place: _____

Please bring a special "heirloom"
that belonged to one of your ancestors.
Be prepared to share a story about
your ancestor and the item you chose.

——

Divine Nature

VALUE EXPERIENCE

This Is Your Life!

On your own: Study the object lesson "This Is Your Life!" on the following page. Do you feel this accurately reflects your goals and priorities? Is it true that we often let the drifts of sand fill up all our time, so that important things are neglected? As you prepare to present this object lesson

- Gather the supplies.
- Check to see that they all fit!
- Practice what you'll say as you explain the concepts.

With your family: Present this object lesson for family home evening. Discuss your busy lives, and make a list of family priorities. Post this list!

For a Young Women or YW/YM activity or class: Ask your Sunday School teacher or Young Women leader to help arrange an appropriate time for this special demonstration. Many gospel lessons can be enhanced with this visual presentation. Arrange a time and prepare the materials for the space available.

GOALS: Recognize that daily choices and priorities will affect you eternally.

Resolve to make time every day for the most important things.

TIME: 30 minutes to learn and practice demonstration several times

HANDOUT: "This Is Your Life!" object lesson outline on page 27

SUPPLIES: Quart jar
2 c. sand
1½ c. beans
5 rocks, about 3" long
Sieve and bowl

HINT: Be sure to practice, and make any needed measurement adjustments; otherwise, your point will be lost.

THIS IS YOUR LIFE!
Object Lesson

1. This **jar** represents our lives. Put **sand** in the jar to represent the many small tasks and events we do each day. For example:
- Wash, dry, and style hair
- Complete chemistry homework
- Go to dentist appointment
- Attend softball practice
- Do dishes, etc.

2. Put **beans** in the jar to represent larger activities and events that take our time. For example:
- Paint bedroom
- Help with birthday party for five-year-old brother
- Travel to California for orchestra performance
- Shop for prom dress
- Prepare for foot surgery, etc.

3. Now put the **large rocks** in the jar, representing life's most important things. Pause to let everyone see that *they don't fit inside!*
Oh no, the really big things don't fit into our lives! We could be spending our days doing only things that the wind can blow away.

4. Start over.
Remove rocks; dump beans and sand through sieve to separate.
Let's put the most important things *first* into our lives.
Have **five individuals** come up, place a **rock** into the jar, and tell a brief example of an eternal value:
- Personal growth
- Family relationships
- Church responsibilities
- Love and service to others
- Relationship with the Savior

These are things of lasting or *eternal* value. They fit in easily.

5. The jar appears almost full. But look! We can still add some other things.
Add **beans**.

6. Is the jar full now?
Add **sand**. Shake and tamp down. Shake some more to make it fit.
It can be hard to get it all in, but we can fit in almost everything if we put the most important things in *first*. We may find that having our priorities in order helps smooth the way as we live each day. In other words, our everyday choices lead to eternal results. "This Is Your Life!"

Divine Nature

VALUE EXPERIENCE

Dried Flower Memories

What can you do with that bouquet of flowers from your best friend? Can you keep the daisies that special guy surprised you with on your birthday, or the long-stemmed roses your proud dad sent after you sang a solo? Here's a great way to make these memories last. Carefully dry the flowers, and then arrange them into a long-lasting floral bouquet to keep you smiling!

With your family: Spend a wonderful hour chatting and working with your mother as you create a lovely "memory bouquet" decoration for your home. Ask your mom about flowers she has received in the past—you may discover something interesting about her life!

How to dry flowers: Tie a string to the bottom of each stem, and hang the flowers upside down in a cool dark place. Hang drying flowers separately or in natural bunches. Try not to bump them, or petals may fall off. Leave undisturbed for several weeks, and then bring out into the light and arrange as desired.

GOALS: Learn a beautiful way to preserve the memory of a wonderful event in your life.

Create a lovely display to brighten your home.

TIME: 30 minutes to select and hang flowers to dry
2 weeks to wait for them to dry
60 minutes to arrange into a beautiful display

HANDOUT: Journal sheet on page 29

SUPPLIES: Flowers of several types, stems included
String or floss
Dark and quiet space to hang flowers
Pot or vase
Spanish moss
Bow, made from ribbon on original bouquet (optional)

HINT: Roses dry especially well. Flowers with just one row of petals, such as daisies, are more fragile. Tiny flowers on multi-branched stems, such as lavender, are lovely when dried. White flowers will turn a bit brown. Brightly colored flowers tend to keep a fresher look.

Dried Flower Memories

Flower Arrangement Record:

FLOWER	EVENT	GIVEN BY

Divine Nature

VALUE EXPERIENCE

Sing of the Savior

Let music help you feel the presence of the Savior in your life.

On your own: Study and learn the lyrics of the song "Come to the Savior" on pages 40–43 of this book. Ask someone to play the music as you sing the words. Be more aware of Jesus Christ as your Savior and brother, who lifts you through His love and example.

With your family: Learn and sing this song for a family home evening. Plan a special family group testimony meeting on a hilltop just at sunset.

As a Young Women's group: Learn and sing "Come to the Savior" as a choir in Young Women meetings. This song has two melody parts that are first sung separately, and then at the same time, creating easy and beautiful harmony. The words emphasize the gift the Savior gave each of us, allowing us to be filled with strength and peace.

GOALS: Better understand the role of Jesus Christ in the plan of salvation.

Choose to accept the gift of forgiveness from your loving brother.

TIME: 30–60 minutes to learn and sing the song several times

HANDOUTS: Music for the song "Come to the Savior" on pages 40–43

SUPPLIES: Copies of the music
Singers divided into two groups
Piano and pianist

HINT: Ask Young Women leaders to help schedule this song for a Young Women's group to sing at New Beginnings, Young Women in Excellence, a fireside, or other special event.

PROJECT: You can expand this activity into a Value Project by leading and directing a Young Women choir as they prepare and perform this song:

DIVINE NATURE VALUE PROJECT
Teach a Song: "Come to the Savior," p. 38

Divine Nature

Mother and Daughter Match-up

For a Young Women activity: With approval from your Young Women leaders, plan and organize a mother/daughter evening. Invite the mothers of all the young women to come with their daughters to this special event. (See invitation on page 33.) Every mom and daughter team should wear a matching outfit—anything from bridal party dresses to matching T-shirts with jeans! They could even style their hair the same. This will be an unforgettable evening for both daughters and mothers.

Preparation: Set up tables and chairs to form a wide front and center aisle for the fashion show. Place strands of tiny white lights along the modeling "runway" and tape into position. Use spotlights if available. Cover tables with pretty tablecloths and add a centerpiece to each. Centerpieces could be flowers in small vases, candles in pretty holders, or antique dolls. Decorate the walls and doorways with swags of tulle topped with silk flowers.

Fashion show: Play lively music as each mother-and-daughter team models their look-alike outfits. Have them parade up the aisle, slowly turn, pose, and then walk back. Award creative prizes to recognize each mother and daughter team, for example: Perfect Match, Craziest Costumes, or Blinding Smiles!

HINT: Be sure to take photographs, or better yet, make a video for everyone to watch at the end of this magical and hilarious evening.

Program: Next on the evening's agenda is a talent show, starring the mothers and daughters. (For a hilarious and super easy non-talent show, check out the "Random Talent Show" in *Midweek Treasures for Young Women* by Jeanni Gould. You simply draw a slip of paper from a jar, and immediately perform whatever the paper tells you, as creatively as possible! For example, "I am a professional air guitarist; do not try this at home.") A guest speaker could also be invited to discuss the challenges and blessings of motherhood.

Refreshments: Top off the event with a delicious dessert.

GOALS: Help to increase the bonds of friendship between mothers and daughters in your ward.

Learn leadership skills as you make arrangements for this event.

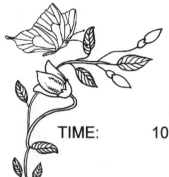

Mother and Daughter
Match-up
(CONTINUED)

TIME: 10+ hours, including time to
- Make arrangements with Young Women leaders
- Schedule the building on the date selected
- Prepare invitations
- Distribute invitations
- Plan and prepare decorations
- Organize materials for talent show
- Shop for ingredients and prepare dessert
- Set up and decorate the room for the event
- Oversee the evening's activities
- Clean up

HANDOUTS: Invitation on page 33
Copies of "Random Talent Show" handouts from *Midweek Treasures for Young Women* (Props List, p. 55; Talents List, p. 56)

SUPPLIES: Matching outfits, supplied by each mother/daughter team
Invitations
Tables and chairs
Tablecloths
Centerpieces
Strands of white lights
Duct tape
Extension cords
Decorations for the room
Microphone (optional)
Music and CD or tape player
Talent list, see *Midweek Treasures for Young Women,* book or CD–ROM (optional)
Props for "Random Talent Show" as listed in above book (optional)
Camera and film, or video camera and player
Dessert as desired
Ice water
Paper supplies: plates, forks, cups, and napkins

HINT: Consider working with another young woman to accomplish this Value Project. You could spend many enjoyable hours coordinating this event together!

VALUE EXPERIENCE: Young women can participate in this special event as a Divine Nature Value Experience.

Mother and Daughter Match-up

A Special Evening for
Mothers and Daughters

Date: _____

Time: _____

Place: _____

Be sure to dress alike!

Mother and Daughter Match-up

A Special Evening for
Mothers and Daughters

Date: _____

Time: _____

Place: _____

Be sure to dress alike!

Divine Nature

VALUE PROJECT

Grandparents' Stories

Begin a family history by gathering several stories from each of your grandparents, or even great-grandparents if you are lucky enough to know them. Tape-record your grandparents as they tell stories in response to your questions. Then transcribe each tale into a computer file, print up copies, and collect all the pages together into a book. Include a Family History sheet (found on page 34) about each grandparent.

Topics that may elicit wonderful stories:
- Earliest memories
- Experience where he or she felt the Holy Ghost
- Story of how each grandparent met and fell in love with his or her spouse
- Memories of great-grandparents
- Funny story about *your* mom or dad as a child

You may want to add a few photographs of each of your grandparents. This will add interest for readers, especially in generations to come. Have someone take a photo of you and your grandparents as you work together on this family history!

With your family: Work closely with your parents and grandparents as you learn more about their lives. They will love helping along the way and will be thrilled to see your marvelous finished project!

GOALS: Gain greater appreciation for your immediate ancestors.

Demonstrate your love to your grandparents through giving them your undivided attention and time.

Prepare a family history that will someday be cherished by your own children.

TIME: 30–60 minutes to record each grandparent, a total of 2–4 hours
8–10 hours to transcribe the stories from the tape
1 hour to print pages and organize into a book

Grandparents' Stories
(CONTINUED)

HANDOUT: Family History sheet to fill in personal information on page 36

SUPPLIES: Tape recorder
Microphone
Tape for each person you will be recording
Labels for tapes (very important)
Computer with word processing program and printer
Printing paper (decorative scrapbook paper optional)
Copy of Family History sheet for each grandparent
Photographs (optional)

For a book:
Loose-leaf binder
Plastic page protectors

For a professionally bound book:
Front and back covers
Binding—quickly accomplished at copy center (approx $3)

HINTS: It takes longer to type from a spoken tape than you expect. Be patient as you stop and rewind a million times. It will be worth it!

Don't wait too long; catch them while their memories are still sharp!

My great-grandmother Lydia Hepworth

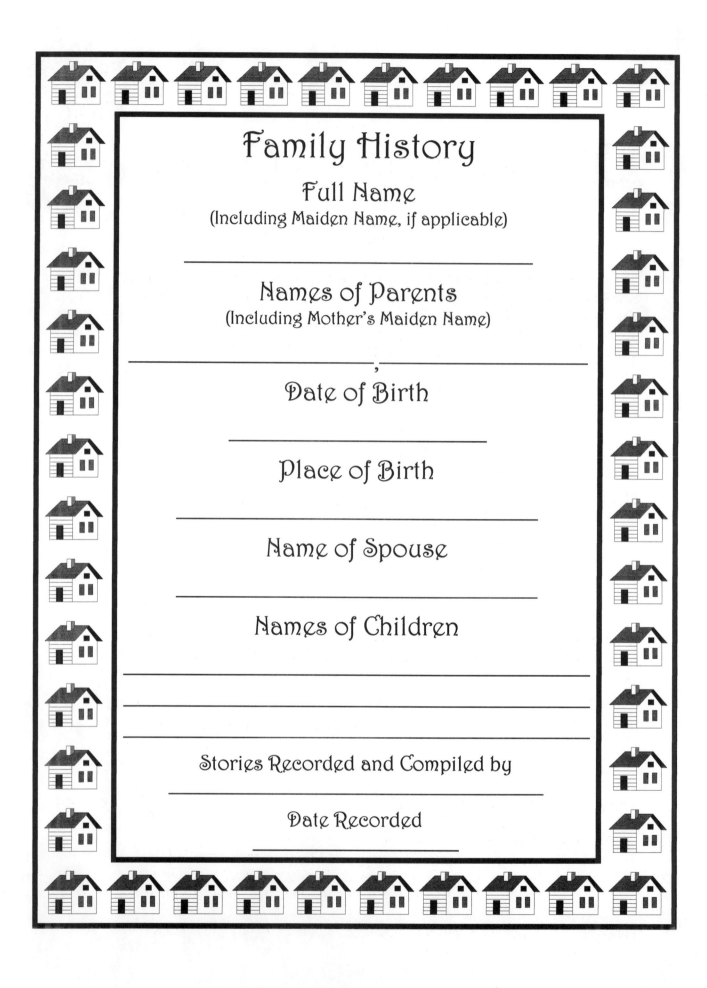

Family History

Full Name
(Including Maiden Name, if applicable)

_____

Names of Parents
(Including Mother's Maiden Name)

_____ , _____

Date of Birth

_____

Place of Birth

_____

Name of Spouse

_____

Names of Children

_____

_____

_____

Stories Recorded and Compiled by

_____

Date Recorded

_____

Divine Nature

I Can't Believe I Cleaned the Whole House!

Clean the entire house—top to bottom and front to back! The knowledge and satisfaction you'll gain from accomplishing this enormous task will help prepare you to become independent—and that time is coming sooner than you or your parents realize! With advice from your mother or other experienced homemaker, make a plan of attack to achieve this goal. First, list the major tasks involved:

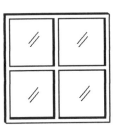

- Scrub all bathrooms
- Clean kitchen counters and sinks
- Shake all throw rugs
- Sweep and mop floors
- Vacuum all carpets
- Dust or polish all furniture and shelves

And then add tasks that may be optional, depending on the time available:

- Vacuum or wipe windowsills
- Dust floorboards and door frames
- Polish wood on cabinets in kitchen and baths
- Clean light fixtures and fans
- Dust window blinds

Gather all cleaning supplies. Following the order suggested above, jump right in! Consider working for five hours the first day, three hours the second, and then two hours the final day. This is an excellent project for those "lazy days of summer!"

GOALS: Prepare to care for your belongings and your future home.

Help improve your home environment right now.

TIME: 10+ hours

SUPPLIES: Willing attitude
Cleaning supplies, as suggested by your mother or father
Basket, to gather up family members' stuff that's in your way
Lively music as you work, to energize your body and mind

HINT: Warn your family in advance, so they can tidy personal areas.

Divine Nature

VALUE PROJECT

Teach a Song: "Come to the Savior"

With approval from your Young Women leaders, learn and then help teach the new song "Come to the Savior" to a group of young women. Arrange an opportunity for them to perform as a choir.

LEARN: Study and learn the lyrics of the song "Come to the Savior" on pages 40–43 of this book. Ask someone to play the piano as you sing the words. The song has a catchy gospel rhythm and is easy to learn.

TEACH: After you are familiar with the song, you can begin to teach it to others. You may want to ask an experienced musician in your ward to assist. This song has two separate melodies that are sung individually, and then sung simultaneously to create an easy and beautiful harmony. At the first rehearsal, have everyone learn both melodies. Then at later practices divide the young women into two groups, including one group of girls who are good at reading music. They will sing the alto part on the last page of the song.

PERFORM: Choose a performance date about six weeks ahead, to allow time to polish all parts. Direct, or arrange for someone to lead, the young women's group as they sing "Come to the Savior" for your ward's sacrament meeting or other special occasion.

GOALS: Better understand the role of Jesus Christ in the plan of salvation.

Increase leadership skills as you make arrangements, teach, and lead rehearsals and performances.

Follow through with your commitment, even if others are not always dependable.

Teach a Song:
"Come to the Savior"
(CONTINUED)

TIME: 10+ hours, including time to
- Study the lyrics and understand the message of the song
- Sing and play through the song several times
- Arrange with leaders for dates to teach it to young women
- Copy and organize sheet music
- Learn how to teach and direct music
- Notify and remind choir members of practice times
- Arrange performance date with ward leaders
- Plan, set up space, and lead musical rehearsals
- Warm up and perform

HANDOUTS: Music for the song "Come to the Savior" on pages 40–43

SUPPLIES: Copies of the music for all young women
Music folders (optional but gives an elegant look as you perform)
Person who is knowledgeable about music and willing to teach you
Singers divided into two groups
Piano and pianist
Calendar to check dates
Treats (optional but rewarding at the end of song practice)

HINT: To include all your ward's young women in your
choir, ask your Young Women leaders if they will
allow you to teach and to practice the music
during opening exercises on Sundays. Be sure to
schedule in advance which Sundays you may rehearse.
Be careful to stick to the time limit they give you.

VALUE EXPERIENCE:
Young women can accomplish a Value Experience as they
participate in this singing group:

DIVINE NATURE VALUE EXPERIENCE
Sing of the Savior, p. 30

Come to the Savior

(Song in Two Parts)

Words & Music by
Jeanni Hepworth Gould

Strongly, ♩ = 144

(Alto)

Come to the Sav - ior, ye heav - y lad - en,

He will give com - fort and bless - ed re - lief;

Lay down your bur - den on His broad shoul - der,

He will give mer - cy, He will bring peace.

Isaiah 9:6

41

42

43

INDIVIDUAL WORTH

Individual Worth

VALUE EXPERIENCE

Create a Collage

On your own: Look through magazines, advertisements, and newspapers to find things that interest you and that reflect your abilities, characteristics, and personal goals. Cut out words, phrases, and pictures in various shapes, colors, and sizes. Arrange these cutouts on a poster board, and then carefully glue one piece at a time onto the board. Display your personal collage proudly in your home.

For a Young Women activity: Working side by side, each young woman can create a personal collage. The young women will then share with each other some of the most interesting pictures or words they chose to describe themselves. Display collage artwork for a short time in the Young Women's room or on a bulletin board at the church. Young women may then take their collages to hang on their walls at home.

GOALS: Recognize your own talents and abilities; you are of great worth.

Create an artistic record of your interests and goals.

TIME: 1 hour

SUPPLIES: Magazines
            Newspapers
            Glue
            Scissors
            Poster board

> Goals   Talents
>
> It's all about me!
>
>   Dreams

HINT: Locate and cut out each of the letters that will spell your name, and then glue these across the poster.

Individual Worth

Self-Esteem Skit

For a Young Women activity: With absolutely no rehearsal needed, invite six young women to perform a two-part skit, "What's in the Center of Your Life?" The script is included on the following page of this book. The skit's message will help motivate you to recenter your life on what is important. This skit is appropriate for any Mutual activity or as a visual presentation to enhance a lesson. Young women could present the skit, and then listen to a guest speaker for a combined lesson on the fifth Sunday of a month.

Illustration 1: Draw a circle to represent Erin, a young woman. Then draw overlapping circles to represent each of the following categories: friends, family, school, and guys—a category by themselves! (See Illustration 1 on page 48.)

Scene One: Six "actors" present the first version of the skit.

Illustration 2: Now redraw the circle for Erin, putting a large circle representing Jesus Christ in the center of her circle. The other circles for friends, etc., come into the edges of the young woman's circle, but they do not fill up the center. (See Illustration 2 on page 48.)

Scene Two: The six actors then re-act the play, with all the speakers saying exactly the same thing. The only change will be Erin's response. Knowing she is a beloved daughter of God and has a special mission here on Earth will help Erin maintain her sense of confidence and self-worth even if others let her down.

GOAL: Recognize that you are of great worth, and able to cope in difficult situations with intelligence and confidence.

TIME: 30 minutes

HANDOUTS: Script for "What's in the Center of Your Life?" skit on page 47
     Illustrations on page 48

SUPPLIES: Copy of script for each actor
     Chalkboard or whiteboard and colored chalk or markers
     (2) "I Am Wonderful!" signs, each hung on piece of string
     Piece of paper with a large *C* written on it
     Copies of illustrations page, to hand out at the conclusion

HINT: In scene two of the skit, Erin can get help from the audience as she creates her own positive responses to each situation.

What's in the Center of Your Life?

ACTORS: Erin   Cynthia   Jessica   Justin
          Mom   Mr. Olson   Narrator (draws graphics and conclusions)

SCENE ONE

Erin, wearing an "I Am Wonderful" sign around her neck, tries a new hairstyle.
Mom: You're not going with your hair like that, are you?

Erin: I know I look ugly, and I have a new zit on my nose. I hate how I look. *TEARS OFF PIECE OF "I AM WONDERFUL" SIGN SHE IS WEARING.*

Cynthia, *calling on the phone:* Erin, I know I said I was going to give you a ride today, but Dana and Samantha—you know those senior girls—just offered to pick me up! So, I'm sorry, but I guess I'll see you at school. Oh, they're here, see you, bye! *Hangs up.*

Erin: Great! And she'll probably ditch me at lunch too. *TEARS OFF PIECE OF SIGN.*

Mr. Olson, *holding out test paper:* Erin, here's your latest geometry test back. You got a C. Not up to your usual standard. Maybe you should spend a little less time with your friends and more time on your studying.

Erin: Yeah, like I have any friends. And now I'm stupid too. I'll never even graduate. *TEARS OFF ANOTHER PIECE OF THE SIGN.*

Jessica: Erin, I just saw the cast list for the school play. You know that part you auditioned for? You'll never believe it, but Cynthia got the part. And you were the one who convinced her to try out! Too bad.

Erin: I thought I sang so well! I'm never trying out again. *TEARS OFF PIECE OF SIGN.*

Justin: Hey! I didn't see you over there. But you know, I was thinking that we shouldn't spend so much time together. I feel like I kind of need my space, you know? (*He calls over his shoulder,* "Just a minute, Samantha, I'll be right there!") See you later, Erin.

Erin: I love him so much! Now no one will ever care about me! *TEARS OFF THE LAST PIECE OF THE SIGN.*

Narrator: When other people and events are at the center of your life, they may occasionally let you down. You are left feeling empty, lost, and less than wonderful.

SCENE TWO

Exactly the same as scene one, except Erin creates new and positive responses to each situation and doesn't tear the sign up. As the new sign states, she knows she is a wonderful person.

Narrator: Put Christ in the center of your life; He will never let you down. He loves each of you, knowing you for exactly who you really are. You deserve a wonderful life—because you are wonderful!

47

What's in the Center of Your Life?

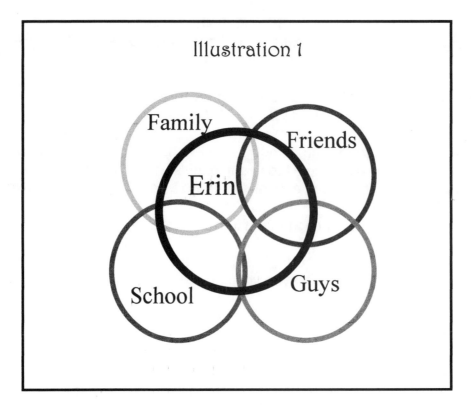

Illustration 1

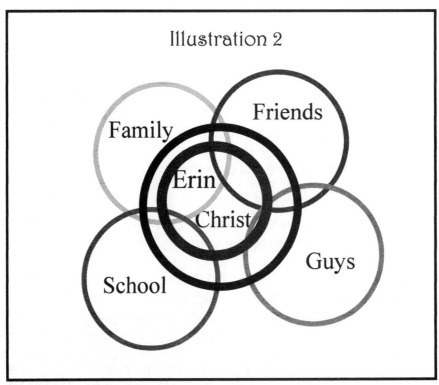

Illustration 2

Individual Worth

VALUE EXPERIENCE

Sing a Song of Gratitude

Congratulations! You've been given the gift of song. The Lord counseled us to *"seek ye earnestly the best gifts, always remembering for what they are given" (D&C 46:8).* The gift of music is so easy to share, and your love of music can help you to lift others.

On your own: Study and learn the lyrics of the song "Gifts" on pages 60–62 of this book. Play, or ask someone to play the music, as you sing the words.

With your family: Learn and sing this song for family home evening. Easy introductory activity: write each family member's name on a separate piece of paper. Pass the papers around and ask everyone to write down one or two gifts that they feel each person has. You will create a list of gifts for each family member. Read each list aloud, so all can see the positive traits others notice in each other.

As a Young Women's group: Learn and sing "Gifts" as a choir in Young Women meetings. Did you notice that part of the melody echoes an old Amish folk song " 'Tis a Gift to Be Simple"? This reminds us to be humble and willing to serve others with our gifts from God.

GOALS: Recognize that you have been given gifts from God.

           Be willing to develop and use those gifts to serve others.

TIME: 30-60 minutes to learn and sing the song several times

HANDOUTS: Music for the song "Gifts" on pages 60–62

SUPPLIES: Copies of the music
           Singers divided into two groups
           Piano and pianist

HINT: Love to perform? Ask Young Women leaders to help schedule this song as a special musical number.

PROJECT: You can expand this activity into a Value Project by directing a Young Women choir as they prepare and perform this song:

INDIVIDUAL WORTH VALUE PROJECT
Teach a Song: "Gifts," p. 58

49

Individual Worth

Appreciating Parents

On your own: Reflect on the qualities you most admire in your mother and your father. Try to identify two or three positive characteristics that you may have inherited from each parent. Write a letter to your mother and a separate letter to your father expressing your appreciation for their excellent qualities. Tell your parents why you are grateful to be blessed with some of their positive traits. Describe to your mother and father several ways that you plan to develop these good qualities.

With your father and mother: Personally give the letter you have written to each parent. Add a hug.

GOALS: Identify positive characteristics of your parents that you may have inherited.

Make a plan to develop these good qualities; begin this plan immediately.

Increase your appreciation for your mother and your father.

TIME: 30–60 minutes

HANDOUT: Decorative stationery on page 51

SUPPLIES: Stationery and pen

HINTS: Ask your father and mother what character traits they feel you may have inherited. Their answers may surprise you!

Try to be only positive as you contemplate your parents' qualities.

Individual Worth

VALUE EXPERIENCE

My Favorite Things

With your family: Plan a special family home evening. Ask each family member in advance to bring one object that is special to him or her. Sitting in a circle, take turns displaying the item each individual selected to bring. Ask each person to explain why this object is one of his or her favorite things.

For a Young Women activity: Invite young women in advance to bring to the activity one object that has particular meaning for her. Ask each girl to keep her item hidden in a brown paper bag as she arrives so no one can see what it is. Invite the young women to sit in a large circle, and place all the "mystery" bags in the center. The young women leader should also contribute a favorite object in a bag to this pile. The leader randomly selects one bag from the group, opens it, and asks the girls to try to guess who brought that particular item.

After the owner is identified, that particular young woman explains why she chose that item as one of her favorite things. She then selects a new bag from the circle's center and opens it, and everyone attempts to guess who owns the special item inside. Continue until everyone has had the opportunity to share.

GOALS: Select one item that is special to you personally, and be able to explain why it is meaningful.

Learn and begin to appreciate particular attributes or interests of each person in your family or young women group.

TIME: 30–60 minutes

HANDOUT: Invitation on page 53

SUPPLIES: Invitations
Brown paper bag and object, brought by each individual

BONUS: At the end of the activity, you can bring out one more paper bag to share—with surprise treats inside!

HINT: This game is a fun and easy way to become more familiar with others in the group. Play My Favorite Things with new Beehives!

My Favorite Things

Date: _____
Time: _____
Place: _____

Please bring something that is special to you!
Note: Keep your treasure hidden in a
brown paper bag until time to share.

My Favorite Things

Date: _____
Time: _____
Place: _____

Please bring something that is special to you!
Note: Keep your treasure hidden in a
brown paper bag until time to share.

Individual Worth

VALUE EXPERIENCE
Tradition!

With your family: Gather together for a special family home evening. Ask each family member to write down at least three things that he or she considers a family tradition. Allow them 8–10 minutes to jog their memories. You may want to bring a calendar for individuals to browse through, as traditional practices are often associated with particular holidays or times of the year.

Ask family members to read their lists aloud. Notice the customs that appear on more than one or two lists: these are definitely traditions for your family! Ask your mother and father whether any of these family customs have been continued from previous generations. Is one side of the family dominant? If so, why do you think that is? Discuss the traditions that you, and each of your siblings, would most like to continue after you are married. Would you be open minded about adopting traditions from your future spouse's family?

Journal: Record in your journal the traditions you would most like to continue in your future family.

GOALS: Gain appreciation for the traditions and customs of your family.

Understand that family traditions can be shared from one generation to the next, and even beyond.

Record in your journal the traditions that will be important for you to continue after you are married and have children of your own.

TIME: 30 minutes

SUPPLIES: Paper and pens
Calendar
Journal

HINT: Consider these examples of family traditions:
On Christmas Eve, act out the story of Jesus' birth
Hike the Grand Canyon each fall
Receive a set of scriptures at your baptism
Use great-grandma's spice cake recipe
Read aloud one chapter of a book each night
Play a certain game on all long drives
Make homemade ice cream for birthdays

Individual Worth

VALUE PROJECT

Get Ready, Get Set, Grow!

Before you know it, you will no longer be living with your parents or have meals prepared for you. Clean clothes will no longer appear like magic and empty Cheerios boxes will no longer be mysteriously replaced through little effort of yours! Are you ready for this? Spend two weeks doing ordinary household tasks on your own. Not only will you master some new skills, but you may also gain a greater appreciation for other family members.

For the next two weeks, take responsibility for the following tasks:
- Do all of your own laundry
- Prepare the grocery lists
- Shop for groceries, keeping within a specified budget (If you do not yet drive, accompany your parent each time he or she shops for food items.)
- Prepare five complete meals for your family, including at least two dinners

With your family: Discuss how your family budgets money. How much do groceries really cost? What is the total price to fill up the gas tank in the car? How much is the water bill each month?

GOALS: Practice skills you will need to become self-sufficient.

Gain insights into some common household tasks, and become more appreciative of those who perform them on a regular basis.

TIME: 10+ hours

SUPPLIES: As recommended by a parent

HINT: Plan meals before you prepare the grocery lists so you can make sure you have the ingredients for your favorite foods!

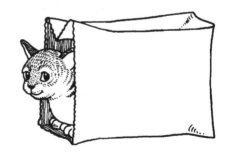

Individual Worth

VALUE PROJECT

Photography Show

Learn and practice the art of photography, and then arrange and exhibit your finest creations.

On your own: Study the principles of photography through a school course or in photography how-to books. Look through the photos you have taken in the past so you can learn from your own experience! Then practice, practice, practice! After each roll of film is taken, develop it immediately and analyze your photos carefully. See how your art is improving?

For a Young Women activity: Arrange to meet with a professional photographer to learn more about his or her art. Ask the photographer to discuss techniques and principles necessary to create excellent photographs.

- Create a pleasing composition:
  Do telephone poles grow out of people's heads? Learn to look beyond your immediate subject and select an appropriate visual frame for the photo. Do you have lots of wasted space in your picture? Have you diminished your picture's impact by including everyone's shoes instead of clearly capturing their glowing faces? Crop your photographs in advance by moving closer to your subjects. Nobody cares about the ceiling!

- Learn about light and shadow:
  Is it better to have your friend squinting into the sun or to have his face blackened out by shadow as the sun shines from behind him? Does everyone have red-eye from the flash? Try to use sources of indirect light. A cloudy day is perfect for portraits! For landscapes, the bright sun at noon will give you harsh photos. Try for early morning or evening to add gorgeous depth and richer colors to your photographs.

- Discover the advantages of various lenses:
  A zoom or close-up lens will focus sharply on your subject while the background will be slightly blurred. This is excellent for portraits—the face will be emphasized and the backdrop will be softened. Discover how a wide-angle lens will allow you to get the whole tower into the picture. This type of lens can also distort angles at the edges of the frame.

- Learn about your camera. Read the owner's manual. Many cameras have special features, such as a fill-in flash or night-mode. Experiment with all your camera's settings!

Photography Show
(CONTINUED)

Prepare your exhibit: Select your most pleasing photographs, focusing on various subjects or one major theme. You may choose to have a few of your very best work enlarged. Mount photos and create a display. Exhibit your work, perhaps in the Young Women's room at the church. Place an announcement in the ward bulletin listing dates and times and inviting ward members to view the photography exhibit.

GOALS: Become an artist as you train your eye to search for the beauty in the world and the people around you.

Share the interesting, exciting, and gorgeous art you have created through photography.

TIME: 2 hours researching photography principles
1 hour reviewing photos (This is fun and may take much longer!)
5 hours composing and snapping pictures in different locations
2 hours preparing exhibit

SUPPLIES: Camera
Various lenses (optional)
Film
Film
More film
Money for photo finishing (this can be expensive)
Rubber cement for mounting photos
Acid-free mounting board or other sturdy material for display
Frames or mat boards (optional)

HINTS: One of the secrets of professional photographers is taking many photos of the same subject, using different distances and angles. Then they only display the one that turned out perfectly!

You may want to document exciting Young Women events through your photography. Be sure to display the finished photos!

Individual Worth

VALUE PROJECT

Teach a Song: "Gifts"

With approval from your Young Women leaders, learn and then help teach the new song "Gifts" to a group of young women. Arrange an opportunity for them to perform as a choir.

LEARN: Study and learn the lyrics of "Gifts" on pages 60–62 of this book. Play the music, or ask someone else to play as you sing the words. Notice that there are two parts: one for sopranos and one for altos. Both parts are very easy to learn and sing. Most of the time everyone sings the melody together. The occasional harmony adds richness to the piece.

TEACH: After you are familiar with the melody and harmony, you can begin to teach it to others. Then divide into two groups; the soprano part will be for young women who enjoy singing high, while the alto part will be for young women who can sing lower. The alto part is best for young women who can read music or are experienced at singing harmony.

PERFORM: Choose a performance date about six weeks ahead, to allow time to polish all parts. Direct the Young Women's group as they sing "Gifts" for Young Women in Excellence or other special occasion.

GOALS: Recognize that everyone has special gifts, given to them by God.

Increase leadership skills as you make arrangements, teach, and lead rehearsals and performances.

Follow through with your commitment, even if others are not always dependable.

HINT: To include all your ward's young women in your choir, ask your Young Women leaders if they will allow you to teach and to practice the music during opening exercises on Sundays. Be sure to schedule in advance which Sundays you may rehearse. Be careful to stick to the time limit they give you.

Teach a Song: "Gifts"
(CONTINUED)

TIME: 10+ hours, including time to
- Study the lyrics and understand the message of the song
- Sing and play through the song several times
- Arrange with leaders for dates to teach it to young women
- Copy and organize the sheet music
- Learn how to teach and direct music
- Notify and remind choir members of practice times
- Arrange performance date
- Plan, set up space, and lead musical rehearsals
- Warm up and perform

HANDOUTS: Music for the song "Gifts" on pages 60–62

SUPPLIES: Copies of the sheet music for all young women
Music folders (optional but looks professional as you perform)
Person who is knowledgeable about music and willing to teach you
Singers divided into two groups
Piano and pianist
Calendar to check dates
Treats (optional but rewarding at the end of song practice)

HINT: Give those with particular musical gifts the opportunity to sing high, help lead the harmony, or accompany on the piano.

VALUE EXPERIENCE:
Here's a suggestion all the singers will appreciate:

INDIVIDUAL WORTH VALUE EXPERIENCE
Sing a Song of Gratitude, p. 49

Gifts

Words & Music by
Jeanni Hepworth Gould
Adapted from Amish folk tune

in my heart from be-fore my birth, I brought a cer-tain tal-ent to the earth; A

bless-ed gift from my Fath-er a-bove, a re-flec-tion of His love.

The mag-ic of mel-o-dy and song that I hear, lifts my heart with joy to
The warmth of a smile giv'n to all that I see, helps me share the gift of

Doctrine & Covenants: 46:10-26

feel the Sa - vior near; To share the mes - sage of the truths I know, sing - ing
love He gave to me; A lis - tening heart and a gen - tle hand show the

sweet - ly through my soul. The more I give, the
kind - ness of a friend.

more my gift will grow; the more I teach, the more I know; the more I serve, the

more I see all the Lord would have me be,

With -

61

in my heart from be - fore my birth, I brought a cer - tain tal - ent to the earth; A di -

vine en - dow - ment from my Fath - er a - bove, a re - flec - tion of His love.

To each a gift from the Lord is giv'n; we

share our gifts to hon - or Him.

KNOWLEDGE

Knowledge

VALUE EXPERIENCE
Art Smart!

Take a tour of your local art museum. Who are your tour guides? Young women in the ward!

Preparation: To prepare for a fun and educational visit to the art museum, make an advance trip to the museum gift store. (Every museum has one!) Purchase a variety of postcards, or a museum catalog, depicting the paintings, sculptures, and other exhibits to be found in the museum. One or two weeks before the museum trip, distribute one museum postcard or illustration from the catalog to each young woman who will be attending. She will become the guide to "her" artwork, with the responsibility to research that particular work and artist.

For a Young Women activity: Travel together to visit the closest art museum. As a group, walk slowly through the museum. All the young women will be eagerly looking at all the displays, searching for "their" works of art. As each young woman recognizes "her" artwork, she'll share what she has learned with the rest of the group.

GOALS: Gain understanding of many great works of art, through personal studying and by listening to others' reports.

Become aware of the great contribution art makes to our world.

TIME: 1 hour to research artwork
90 minutes to visit museum

SUPPLIES: Postcards, brochures, or a catalog from the art museum

HINTS: Many museums have one day each week where admission is free!

Follow up by inviting young women to share artwork they have created. Set up a display at your ward.

PROJECT: Excited about art? Consider this Value Project:

INDIVIDUAL WORTH VALUE PROJECT
Photography Show, p. 56

Knowledge

VALUE EXPERIENCE
Memory Hymn

No need to hum your favorite hymn—you know all the words! One of the first tasks given to Emma Smith, wife of the Prophet Joseph, was to make a collection of hymns for Church members to sing. (See Doctrine & Covenants 25:11–13.) Learning and singing a hymn of Zion will help to strengthen your testimony of the Savior. The words and melody will remain with you forever. Put the incredible power of music to work in a positive way in your life. Music touches our hearts and helps to bring the Spirit very near.

On your own: Study and learn the words to all the verses of one of your favorite hymns. Here are some suggested hymns to learn:

"The Spirit of God" #2	"Where Can I Turn for Peace?" #129
"Be Still, My Soul" #124	"A Poor Wayfaring Man of Grief" #29
"I Believe in Christ" #134	"As Zion's Youth in Latter Days" #256
"I Stand All Amazed" #193	"As Now We Take the Sacrament" #169

With your family: For family home evening, sing all the verses of the song you have chosen. Invite each family member to choose a favorite hymn, and then sing each song together.

Follow up: Ask Young Women leaders if the youth can sing the hymn you have memorized for opening exercises on Sunday or at a Mutual activity night.

GOALS: Remember forever the gospel principles illustrated in this hymn.

Appreciate the power and significance of music in your life. Resolve to choose wisely the music you listen to.

TIME: 30–60 minutes to learn and sing the song several times.

SUPPLIES: Hymn book
Piano (optional)
Tape recorder and tape (optional)

HINT: Tape-record the song as you sing it all the way through, and then listen to the tape as you do homework, travel in the car, etc. This will make it easy to memorize.

Knowledge

VALUE EXPERIENCE

Library Scavenger Hunt

Your local library is an enormous treasure chest. Open the lid to new knowledge as you explore!

For a Young Women activity: Visit the nearest library and browse together through the riches of books and information. Get a deeper look into what is available as you each try to be the first to finish the Library Scavenger Hunt. Girls will fill in the answers to each part of the quest as they quickly and *very quietly* compete to complete the list.

With your family: This activity would also work well for a family home evening. Invite a few friends to increase the intellectual competition!

GOALS: Increase your knowledge of how to research any subject.

               Get excited about reading great books!

TIME: 1 hour

HANDOUT: Library Scavenger Hunt list on page 67

SUPPLIES: Copies of the list
                Pencils

HINT: The Library Scavenger Hunt is a good opportunity to recall and review delightful picture books!

66

Library Scavenger Hunt

1. What is the earliest time the library is open? _____

2. Write the headline from The New York Times for today:

_____

3. Name the topic that is numbered 595.78: _____

4. Does your library still have those little wooden card file drawers?
Circle one: YES   NO

5. Search in the computer (or card file) for the book *Goodnight Moon*,
and write the name of the author: _____

6. Explore the picture book area of the library. Find and write down
the title of a picture book you remember reading *more than once:*

_____

7. How many copies of plays by William Shakespeare are on the
shelf in the library right now? _____

8. Is there a movie on video here in the library that you own at home?
Circle one: YES   NO

9. How much does it cost to make one letter-size photocopy? _____

10. In what library section would you find a book by Isaac Asimov?

_____

11. Write down three book titles by the author L. M. Montgomery.

_____,_____,_____

12. What Dewey decimal number would you look under for a book
about the planet Jupiter? _____

Knowledge

VALUE EXPERIENCE

Sing a Song of Strength

"Who can find a virtuous woman? For her price is far above rubies."
(Proverbs 31:10).

On your own: Study and learn the lyrics of the song "A Woman of Virtue" on pages 76–78 of this book. Play or ask someone to play the music as you sing the words.

With your family: Learn and sing this song for a special family home evening. Read Proverbs 31 together. This chapter illuminates many attributes of a good woman. Discuss which verses describe each family member most closely.

As a Young Women's group: Learn and sing "A Woman of Virtue" as a choir in Young Women meetings. There are two parts: soprano and alto. Both parts are easy to learn and sing. Most of the time everyone sings the melody together. The occasional harmony adds richness to the song.

GOALS: Choose one of the traits described in the song that you wish to develop in yourself.

Commit to prepare now to be a valuable asset to the Lord's kingdom.

TIME: 30–60 minutes to learn and sing the song several times

HANDOUTS: Music for the song "A Woman of Virtue" on pages 76–78

SUPPLIES: Copies of the music
Singers divided into two groups
Piano and pianist

HINT: Check with your leaders to schedule a date to sing this song as a Young Women's group for a special musical number.

PROJECT: You can expand this activity into a Value Project by leading and directing a Young Women's choir as they prepare and perform this song:

KNOWLEDGE VALUE PROJECT
Teach a Song: "A Woman of Virtue," p. 74

Knowledge

VALUE EXPERIENCE

School Is Cool

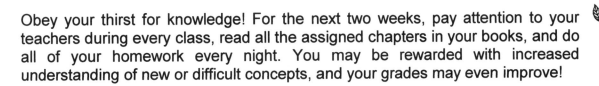

Obey your thirst for knowledge! For the next two weeks, pay attention to your teachers during every class, read all the assigned chapters in your books, and do all of your homework every night. You may be rewarded with increased understanding of new or difficult concepts, and your grades may even improve!

Tell your friends that you intend to listen carefully to the teachers. Ask for your friends' support and cooperation. You won't be able to write notes or talk during class, but you can do this before or after school. In the evenings you may talk on the phone with a clear conscience—knowing your homework is already completed!

GOALS: Gain as much knowledge as possible, using your educational opportunities to the fullest.

Learn an effective technique to achieve academic excellence.

TIME: Two weeks of regular school time

HINT: An easy way to be more attentive in class is by choosing to sit in the front row. If you have assigned seating, you may benefit from requesting a closer desk. Teachers will appreciate your desire to do your best in school.

Knowledge

VALUE EXPERIENCE
Fancy Folds

Discover a delightful way to decorate your table for every meal. Create a beautiful napkin fold called bird-of-paradise. This folding design actually does look like the tropical flower bird-of-paradise. Fancy-folded napkins will make you feel you are dining in an exquisite restaurant!

On your own: Gain skill as you learn and practice the fancy napkin pattern bird-of-paradise. Follow the simple step-by-step instructions on the following page. Fold a napkin for each member of your family. Set the table correctly, adding candles, a centerpiece, and the fancy-folded napkins. Place a napkin in the center of each dinner plate, or just above the plate, so that you can see the bird-of-paradise silhouette. Enjoy the compliments!

For a Young Women activity: Learn five or more beautiful napkin folds. Ask an expert (someone who has read a book on the subject) to demonstrate. All the young women can follow along step by step as they learn a variety of folds. Using different sets of cloth napkins, young women can create many folded designs and be able to show off their results as a fancy display! For example, all the young women could fold pink napkins into seashell designs, gold napkins into bird-of-paradise designs, large white napkins into fleur-de-lis folds, etc.

GOALS: Learn and practice a skill to dress up your table settings at no cost.

                Be willing or even eager to set the table for your family.

TIME: 15 minutes to learn and practice the bird-of-paradise fold
                1 hour to work on a variety of folds for an activity

HANDOUT: Bird-of-paradise napkin folding instruction sheet on page 71

SUPPLIES: Bird-of-paradise instruction sheet
                Square cloth napkins, preferably 15" or larger
                Napkin-folding book, available at your local library

HINT: Girls could fold fancy napkins for a special event:

DIVINE NATURE VALUE PROJECT
Mother and Daughter Match-up, p. 31

CHOICE AND ACCOUNTABILITY VALUE PROJECT
Pretty for Prom, p. 87

Bird-of-Paradise

NAPKIN FOLDING INSTRUCTIONS

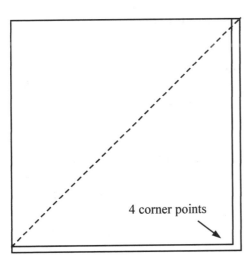

1. Fold napkin into quarters so it forms a square. Then take corner with four open points and fold napkin up diagonally in half.

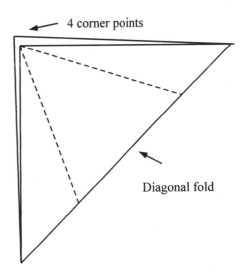

2. Napkin should form a triangle. Then, holding one finger at four corner points, fold sides down along dotted lines. There will be little pointed flaps hanging over the diagonal fold.

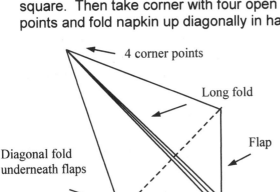

3. Holding napkin folds in place, carefully turn it over. The little pointed flaps will peek out from underneath. Fold pointed flaps up over the napkin.

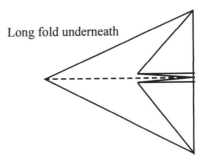

4. Holding pointed flaps in place, fold entire napkin in half so flaps are *inside.*

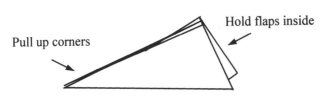

5. Hold flap edge firmly closed between right thumb and fingers (right side in illustration above). With left hand, pull up the four separate corners, one at a time, from inside the top long edge of the napkin. These corners form the pointed petals of the flower.

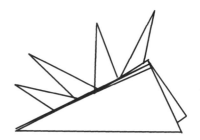

6. Finished bird-of-paradise fold will stand up on its own.

Knowledge

VALUE PROJECT

Prophet's Biography

Read a biography of one of the greatest men on earth: a prophet of the Lord. As you read, liken the prophet's experiences to those in your own life and in the lives of your parents or grandparents.

With your family: Share several interesting stories from the life of the prophet you have chosen to study. Discuss how your family can follow that prophet.

GOALS: Trace the path of righteous choices made by one of the Lord's modern prophets.

Resolve to heed the words and to emulate the actions of this great man.

TIME: 10+ hours

SUPPLIES: Choose one of the following biographies:
Go Forward with Faith: The Biography of President Gordon B. Hinckley
        By Sheri L. Dew
Ezra Taft Benson: A Biography
        By Sheri L. Dew
Howard W. Hunter: Biography of a Prophet
        By Eleanor Knowles
Harold B. Lee: Prophet and Seer
        By L. Brent Goates

HINT: Do you notice that much of the information in the book is taken from the actual journal entries of the prophet? Be inspired to keep your journal writing meaningful and up to date!

VALUE EXPERIENCE:
        How can you find time to do so much reading? Try this suggestion:

CHOICE AND ACCOUNTABILITY VALUE EXPERIENCE
Turn Off the TV! p. 81

Knowledge

VALUE PROJECT

Sew Cool Pajama Pants!

Work on your sewing skills as you cut and seam together a fun pair of comfy pajama pants with a drawstring waist. Pajama pants are very fashionable these days—and not just for bed!

How to: Select and purchase a simple pattern. If this is your first sewing project, select a style with only three pattern pieces: front, back, and drawstring. Now for the fun part: choose a cute fabric! Choose a material that is inexpensive and also permanent press. (If you pick 100% cotton, you'll have to iron it!) Buy the fabric yardage required for the appropriate size, as stated on the back of the pattern envelope. Following the layout guide, cut out the fabric pieces. Then pin and sew it together step by step according to the pattern directions. Isn't that easy? Model your finished pajama pants for your family and friends!

For a Young Women activity: Your entire class can accomplish a Knowledge Value Project and enjoy encouraging and admiring each other at the same time! Schedule three or four days to hold two-hour sewing sessions. Use the same pattern for all the pajama pants (some patterns even have multiple sizes included in one envelope). Young women can shop for fabric with their mothers. Ask talented mothers to assist at the activities as the young women learn to sew. When all young women have completed their sewing projects, put on some fun music and have them all model their amazing creations! Take lots of photos.

GOAL: Learn and practice the skill of sewing as you create a fun and wearable project!

TIME: 2 hours selecting and buying pattern and fabric
2 hours laying out fabric and pattern pieces and cutting fabric
4-6 hours sewing and pressing seams, and assisting others
2 hours total time spent setting up and cleaning up

SUPPLIES: Pattern
Fabric
Straight pins
Scissors
Cutting board or other flat surface
Thread
Large safety pin, for threading drawstring through casing
Sewing machine(s)
Mother(s) or other sewing expert(s)

Knowledge

VALUE PROJECT

Teach a Song:
"A Woman of Virtue"

With approval from your Young Women leaders, learn and then help teach the new song "A Woman of Virtue" to a group of young women. Arrange an opportunity for them to perform as a choir.

LEARN: Study and learn the lyrics of "A Woman of Virtue" on pages 76–78 of this book. Ask someone to play the music on the piano as you sing the words. Notice that there are two parts: one for sopranos and one for altos. Both parts are very easy to learn and sing. Most of the time everyone sings the melody together. The occasional harmony adds richness to the song.

TEACH: After you are familiar with the melody and harmony, you can begin to teach it to others. First ask everyone to sing the melody all the way through so it becomes familiar. Then divide into two groups; the soprano part will be for young women who enjoy singing high, while the alto part will be for young women who can sing lower. The alto part is best for young women who can read music or are experienced at singing harmony.

As you sing together, notice the magnificent qualities that may describe you as a woman: virtuous, strong, reverent, praiseworthy, seeking knowledge, wise, joyful, caring, Christlike, courageous, filled with light, worth more than precious jewels. All these traits for women are taken directly from Proverbs 31. Read it! Isn't it wonderful to be a woman?

PERFORM: Choose a performance date about six weeks ahead, to allow time to polish all parts. Lead a Young Women's group as they sing "A Woman of Virtue" for New Beginnings, a fireside, or other special event.

GOALS: Learn more of your potential strengths as a woman in the Lord's kingdom.

Increase leadership skills as you make arrangements, teach, and lead rehearsals and performances.

Follow through with your commitment, even if others are not always dependable.

Teach a Song:
"A Woman of Virtue"
(CONTINUED)

TIME: 10+ hours, including time to
- Study the lyrics and understand the message of the song
- Sing and play through the song several times
- Arrange with leaders for dates to teach it to young women
- Copy and organize sheet music
- Learn how to teach and direct music
- Notify and remind choir members of practice times
- Arrange performance date
- Plan, set up space, and lead musical rehearsals
- Warm up and perform

HANDOUTS: Music for the song "A Woman of Virtue" on pages 76–78

SUPPLIES: Copies of the sheet music for all young women choir members
Music folders (optional but gives an elegant look as you perform)
Person who is knowledgeable about music and willing to teach you
Singers divided into two groups
Piano and pianist
Calendar to check dates
Treats (optional)

HINT: To include all your ward's young women in your choir, ask your Young Women leaders if they will allow you to teach and to practice the music during opening exercises on Sundays. Be sure to schedule in advance which Sundays you may rehearse. Be careful to stick to the time limit they give you.

VALUE EXPERIENCE:
Choir members may accomplish a Value Experience as they participate in this group:

KNOWLEDGE VALUE EXPERIENCE
Sing a Song of Strength, p. 68

A Woman of Virtue

Words & Music by
Jeanni Hepworth Gould

1. A wo-man of vir - tue, a wo-man of faith,
2. A wo-man of vir - tue, a wo-man of faith,

a wo-man who re - veres the Lord, re - ceives the Lord's praise.
a wo-man who re - veres the Lord, re - ceives the Lord's praise.

For wis-dom and know - ledge her mind and heart yearn;
She stretch-es her hand out to care for the weak;

Proverbs 31 & Matthew 25

Through search-ing the word of God, His ways she will learn.
Through shar-ing the love of Christ, His ways she will seek.

Plac-ing her trust in the Sav - ior, she seeks for His light_;
Pre-par-ing now for His ser - vice, she's will-ing, she's wise_;

In tri - al she shall not fear, her can-dle shines in the night.
Her heart shall re - joice, re - joice, through all the days of her life.

A wo-man of hon - or, a wo-man of strength___,

a wo-man of vir - tue sent for this day,

rit.

She lifts her lamp be - fore the world,

f Worth more than ru - bies in the king - dom of God.

rit.

molto rit.

CHOICE AND ACCOUNTABILITY

Choice and Accountability

My Own Little Corner

Do you have a spot in your home where you constantly drop stuff? Backpacks, sport bags, mail, books, magazines, hair pins, earrings, papers, and other items may stack up quickly in certain areas as you busily go about your day. It could be your desktop, a kitchen or bathroom countertop, the bottom stair, a hall table, or (gasp!) even your bedroom floor.

On your own: Choose to keep this particular space or area of your home perfectly organized for two weeks. As you take responsibility for creating order in one little corner of your life, you may realize the benefits of being organized in other aspects of your life.

With your family: If you are lucky enough to share a room with your sister, ask her to cooperate in keeping her belongings put away too.

GOALS: Take responsibility for your belongings.

            Appreciate the peace of orderly surroundings.

TIME: 10 minutes daily
            (How much stuff do you have?)

SUPPLIES: A place for everything

BONUS: You'll know where to find the
            items you need in a hurry!

PROJECT: Are you someone who
            appreciates tidiness and order?
            Consider this Value Project:

DIVINE NATURE VALUE PROJECT
I Can't Believe I Cleaned the Whole House! p. 37

Choice and Accountability

VALUE EXPERIENCE
Turn Off the TV!

When you begin this Value Experience, it may seem as though you are living in an alternate universe! For two weeks, do not watch any television. (The exception would be for a specific school assignment.) Do not watch movies, play video or computer games, or use the instant messenger feature on your computer. In addition, dramatically limit your time on the telephone. Yes, that's for two weeks.

How to: The object of this experience is to gather up the hours you may otherwise waste, and put them to positive, productive use! During the time you would normally be watching television or playing on the computer, choose to spend time at the piano practicing and perfecting a new piece—be it "Chopsticks" or Chopin! Read the *New Era* cover to cover. Write in your journal. Organize your treasure drawer. Take your puppy for a walk. Learn to cook a new dish. Read a good book. Start a sewing project with your friend, your sister, or your mom. The ideas are endless! How much time do you really have? Each hour is so valuable; make every one count for your good!

With your family: Do something interesting with members of your family. Make this experience not just time you passed, but time you'll all remember with a smile!

GOALS: Break a negative or time-wasting habit.

            Practice positive skills that will develop your character in the ways you wish to grow.

TIME: Hmmm, tough question! How much time will you *gain?*

SUPPLIES: Will depend on the activities you choose

HINT: Review your feelings and behavior as you complete this Value Experience. You may choose to continue to "Turn Off the TV!"

PROJECT: You can expand this activity into a Value Project by selecting a major goal to accomplish during your free time. For example:

KNOWLEDGE VALUE PROJECT
Sew Cool Pajama Pants! p. 73

Choice and Accountability

VALUE EXPERIENCE

Mystery Brownies

Bake brownies for your family or Young Women's group. Be sure to use one of the special brownie recipes on the following page. Tell the following story, and then offer the treat as you present this surprising object lesson.

With your family or Young Women's group: State that it is often hard to understand why some music, movies, books, and magazines are not acceptable material for us to see, hear, or bring into the home. Tell the following story:

STORY

"Three teenagers wanted to go see a particular PG-13 movie that everyone said was terrific. This movie had their favorite actors. It was only rated PG-13 because of the suggestion of sex—nothing was ever really shown. The language was pretty good—the Lord's name was only used in vain twice in the whole movie. The teens did admit there was a scene where a building and a bunch of people were blown up, but the violence was not graphic. Even Church members said it was great. And, even if there were a few minor negative things, the special effects were fabulous, the character development was really good, and the plot was action packed."

Treat: Ask your family or group if they would like to have one of the brownies you just baked. Then explain that you have taken your family's favorite recipe and added a little something extra. When they ask what ingredient you have added, calmly reply, "A hairy spider." Then quickly reassure them that it is only a little addition! Explain to them that all other ingredients are gourmet quality, and you've taken great care to bake the brownies at the precise temperature for the exact time required. Tell the group you are certain the brownies will be superb. If (when) they continue to refuse your delicious treat, act surprised. After all, it is only one small part that is causing them to be so stubborn. Tell them you are sure they would hardly notice it.

Discussion: In what ways is the movie these teens wanted to see like the tainted brownies? Satan tries to enter our minds and our homes by deceiving us into believing that just a little bit of evil won't matter. But the truth is, even a small spider makes the difference between a great treat and something disgusting and totally unacceptable. Even though the movie industry would have us believe that today's movies are acceptable fare for adults and youth, many are not.

Put the movie you want to see to the test. Are there any ingredients you should reject? Would you be comfortable taking Jesus with you? Or the prophet?

Mystery Brownies
(CONTINUED)

GOALS: Through preparing and teaching this object lesson, learn that we must not allow any evil into our minds.

Commit as a family or group to not see, hear, or allow into our hearts such unacceptable movies, music, or magazines.

TIME: 10 minutes to prepare brownies (not including baking time)
20 minutes to prepare and present object lesson

SUPPLIES: Brownie ingredients as specified in either recipe

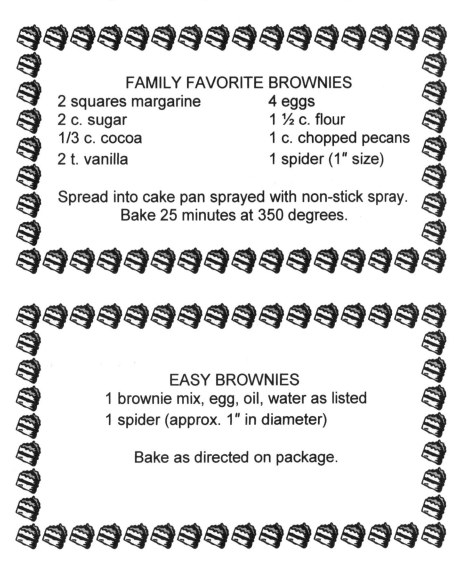

FAMILY FAVORITE BROWNIES

2 squares margarine	4 eggs
2 c. sugar	1 ½ c. flour
1/3 c. cocoa	1 c. chopped pecans
2 t. vanilla	1 spider (1" size)

Spread into cake pan sprayed with non-stick spray.
Bake 25 minutes at 350 degrees.

EASY BROWNIES
1 brownie mix, egg, oil, water as listed
1 spider (approx. 1" in diameter)

Bake as directed on package.

HINT: You will have fun deciding which way to prepare the brownies!!

Choice and Accountability

Sing of the Spirit

You can probably still remember a Primary song about the Holy Ghost. Seek humbly to feel the peace and comfort of the Holy Ghost as you sing this song. You can gain spiritual strength in your life by using the power of music.

On your own: Study and learn the lyrics of the song "A Gentle Touch" on pages 94–97 of this book. Ask someone to play the music as you sing the words.

With your family: Learn to sing this song for a special family home evening. Ask your parents and older siblings to each share a personal experience in which they have been guided or taught by the Holy Ghost.

As a Young Women's group: Learn and sing "A Gentle Touch" as a choir in Young Women meetings. This song has a catchy rhythm and is easy to learn.

As you sing together, notice how the lyrics begin with words from "I Am a Child of God," by Naomi W. Randall and Mildred Pettit. This new song reminds us how the Holy Ghost can continue to lead and guide us as we face many choices on our path back to Heavenly Father.

GOAL: Better understand the role of the Holy Ghost in the great plan of happiness.

TIME: 30–60 minutes to learn and sing the song several times

HANDOUTS: Music for the song "A Gentle Touch" on pages 94–97

SUPPLIES: Copies of the music
           Singers
           Piano and pianist

HINT: Do you like to perform? Ask Young Women leaders to help schedule a date to sing this song as a Young Women's group for a fireside, New Beginnings, or other special event.

PROJECT: You can expand this activity into a Value Project by leading a Young Women choir as they prepare and perform this song.

CHOICE AND ACCOUNTABILITY VALUE PROJECT
Teach a Song: "A Gentle Touch," p. 92

Choice and Accountability

VALUE EXPERIENCE

Listen for Your Life

For a Young Women or YW/YM activity: Use your ears—and your mind—as you play an exciting outdoor game. Play "Listen for Your Life" in the dark and with all players, except three leaders, blindfolded. Although you cannot see, you can listen and follow instructions. The object of the game is to reach the goal safely. This game is great fun, but also dramatically teaches an important lesson for life.

How to play: In a large outdoor open space, blindfolded participants stand in a loose group. Players are not allowed to talk. They listen closely and hear two of the leaders giving brief directions out loud (for example, "Watch out! Go left"). The blindfolded players move silently and carefully toward the person calling them, attempting to reach safety. There is a trick: two different leaders are giving the instructions—in loud voices. The leaders giving these short instructions move around the outer circle of the group, so that their locations change frequently. As the players follow one or another of the leaders, they find themselves constantly changing directions too.

Reaching the goal: The third leader stands perfectly still a little distance away from the group. He or she speaks in a soft steady voice: "Here I am. This is the way. Come toward me." Gradually a few players will begin to hear this quiet voice. As they move toward the voice, they realize that it stays *still*. Players who reach the leader representing the "still, small voice" succeed at the game.

GOAL: Realize that listening to the Holy Ghost can help you navigate the many choices and influences you face as you travel through life.

TIME: 30 minutes

SUPPLIES: Large outdoor area
Blindfolds

Shhh!

Choice and Accountability

VALUE EXPERIENCE

Good News?

Browse through recent newspapers or news magazines. Find five separate reports of terrible events that were caused by bad decisions. Analyze the point where the wrong choices were made. Determine what actions could have been taken to prevent these tragedies. Then search for five news articles that demonstrate examples of good decisions causing positive results.

On your own: Write in your journal some of the choices you must make in the near future. Record your commitment to use the guidelines given to you by the Lord's prophets as you choose your actions in each case.

With your family: Plan a family home evening to discuss the news articles you have found. As a family, resolve to make the kinds of choices that will prevent many tragic happenings. Ask your parents and older siblings to each share a personal experience in which they made a wise and righteous choice.

GOALS: Understand that your decisions can have far-reaching consequences—for good or bad.

Plan now to choose the right when faced with a difficult situation.

TIME: 30–60 minutes

SUPPLIES: Newspapers and magazines
Scissors
Journal and pen

Choice and Accountability

VALUE PROJECT
Pretty for Prom

Is it possible to be beautiful and modest at the same time? Test the limits . . . of your creativity as you arrange a glamorous fashion show for the young women of your ward. Girls become "princesses" for the evening as they arrive in semi-formal dress. The princess theme for this event will remind you that you are a "royal" daughter of God.

For a Young Women activity: With approval from your Young Women leaders, stage a formal fashion show featuring modest options for significant dress-up occasions. You may choose to invite the fathers of all the young women to come with their daughters to this special event. (See invitation on page 89.)

Preparation: Set up tables and chairs to form a wide front and center aisle for the fashion show. Place strands of tiny white lights along the modeling "runway" and tape into position. Arrange spotlights, if available. Cover the tables with pretty tablecloths; create centerpieces with little girl's glittering princess dress-up shoes (draped with brightly colored beaded necklaces); and then sprinkle shiny confetti over the tabletop. Cut out a large royal crown from gold or silver metallic poster board, hang it high on the wall, and drape swags of tulle out from each side of the crown. You may also make a smaller crown-and-tulle drape to create a royal entry at the doorway. Silk trees decorated with white lights can add elegance to the room.

Fashion show: You may invite the Laurels to be models for the evening. Play romantic music as each young woman in turn models a formal gown. Each girl walks gracefully up the aisle, slowly turns, poses, and then walks back, as an announcer describes the marvelous (and modest) features of her dress. (Refer to "For the Strength of Youth" pamphlet as you pre-screen dresses for modesty.)

Photographs: Have a "professional" photographer (see Individual Worth Value Project on page 56) set up a backdrop area and take pictures of your beautiful girls with their fathers. You may choose to place a silk tree decorated with white twinkle lights as part of the background for the photographs.

Program: A guest speaker could be invited to discuss fashion, formals, and how to hold to modest standards. Daughters could also invite their fathers to dance.

Refreshments: Top off the event with a delicious dessert.

Pretty for Prom
(CONTINUED)

GOALS: Help the young women in your ward discover ways to live up to the Lord's standards, even when shopping for formal gowns. Commit to make no compromises in your own apparel.

Learn leadership skills as you make arrangements for this event.

TIME: 10+ hours, including time to
- Make arrangements with Young Women leaders
- Schedule the building for the date selected
- Make and distribute invitations for fathers and daughters
- Plan and prepare decorations
- Shop for ingredients and prepare dessert
- Set up and decorate the room for the event
- Oversee the evening's activities
- Clean up

HANDOUT: Invitation on page 89

SUPPLIES: Invitations
Formal dresses and shoes
Tables and chairs
Tablecloths
Centerpieces
Strands of white lights
Duct tape
Extension cords
Decorations for the room
Microphone (optional)
Music and CD or tape player
Camera and film or video camera
Dessert as desired
Ice water
Paper supplies: plates, forks, cups, and napkins

HINTS: Film a video for everyone to watch at the end of this magical evening.

Consider working with another young woman to accomplish this Value Project. You could spend many enjoyable hours coordinating this event together!

VALUE EXPERIENCE:
For a Choice and Accountability Value Experience, young women may commit to dress appropriately for all the dances they attend.

Formal Dress

Date: _____
Time: _____
Place: _____

Please come to a
Fashion Show
for Fathers and
Daughters!
Featuring "Modest Models"

Pretty
For
Prom

Choice and Accountability

VALUE PROJECT
The Big Payoff

Can I spend my money on a movie now, and still buy that computer? Choose to work steadily toward a larger goal, recognizing that smaller sacrifices may be necessary along the way.

On your own: Set a goal to purchase a substantial item (for example, a CD player, a computer, a varsity letter jacket, or a snowboard). Determine how much money you will need, and then work hard to earn the necessary cash. As you earn money, place it in a special account designated for your major purchase. Keep a record of your goal and of your financial progress along the way. This will help encourage you to continue saving until you reach the full amount needed. Then purchase the item for which you have saved. Feel the satisfaction of accomplishing your goal!

With your family: If you don't have a job, you can likely make arrangements with your parents to earn money doing *extra* jobs around your home. When you explain that you have a long-term goal in mind, they can help and encourage you by offering a variety of work opportunities. Parents know that if you earn it, you will appreciate it! Here are some examples of work you can accomplish for cash:
- Wash the car
- Wash all the windows, inside and out
- Babysit
- Organize closets and cabinets
- Clean the garage
- Prune trees and shrubs (and pick up trimmings)
- Paint the woodwork throughout the house
- Shine all kitchen appliances, inside and out

GOALS: Make financial choices that will benefit you in the long term.

Follow through on your commitment to your goal.

TIME: Will depend on purchase goal

SUPPLIES: Notebook and pen to keep records
Bank account

HINT: Be sure to pay your tithing first!

The Big Payoff

Goal:

$ \$ $ $ \$ $

_____

Cost estimate: _____

Planned purchase date: _____

Savings Record		
$ Amount	Date earned	Type of work

Choice and Accountability

VALUE PROJECT

Teach a Song: "A Gentle Touch"

With approval from your Young Women leaders, learn and then help teach the new song "A Gentle Touch" to a group of young women. Arrange an opportunity for them to perform as a choir.

LEARN: Study and learn the lyrics of the song "A Gentle Touch" on pages 94–97 of this book. Play the music, or ask someone to play as you sing the words. Notice that everyone sings the melody together, except on page four where there is an opportunity for altos to sing harmony. This song has a catchy rhythm and is very easy to learn.

TEACH: After you are familiar with the song, you can begin to teach it to others. You may want to ask a musician in your ward to assist. At the first rehearsal, have everyone learn the melody. Then at later practices divide into two groups, including one group of girls who are especially good at reading music. They will sing the harmony part on page 3 of the song.

As you sing together, notice how the song begins with words from "I Am a Child of God," by Naomi W. Randall and Mildred Pettit. This new song for young women reminds us how the Holy Ghost can continue to lead and guide us as we face many choices on our path back to Heavenly Father.

PERFORM: Choose a performance date about six weeks ahead, to allow time to polish all parts. Lead the Young Women's group as they sing "A Gentle Touch" for your ward's sacrament meeting or another special occasion.

GOALS: Better understand the role of the Holy Ghost in your life.

Increase leadership skills as you make arrangements, teach, and lead rehearsals and performances.

Follow through with your commitment, even if others are not always dependable.

Teach a Song:
"A Gentle Touch"
(CONTINUED)

TIME: 10+ hours, including time to
- Study the lyrics and understand the message of the song
- Sing and play through the song several times
- Arrange with leaders for dates to teach it to young women
- Copy and organize the sheet music
- Learn how to teach and direct music
- Notify and remind choir members of practice times
- Arrange performance date
- Plan, set up space, and lead musical rehearsals
- Warm up and perform

HANDOUTS: Music for the song "A Gentle Touch" on pages 94–97

SUPPLIES: Copies of the music for all choir members
Music folders (optional but adds a classy look)
Person who is knowledgeable about music
Singers divided into two groups
Piano and pianist
Calendar to check dates
Treats (optional but rewarding after song practice)

HINTS: Invite choir members to share examples of when they have felt the influence of the Holy Ghost.

To include all your ward's young women in your choir, ask your Young Women leaders if they will allow you to teach and to practice the music during opening exercises on Sundays. Be sure to schedule in advance which Sundays you may rehearse. Be careful to stick to the time limit they give you.

VALUE EXPERIENCE:
Young women can accomplish a Value Experience as they participate in this singing group:

CHOICE AND ACCOUNTABILITY VALUE EXPERIENCE
Sing of the Spirit, p. 84

A Gentle Touch

Words & Music by
Jeanni Hepworth Gould

Gently, ♩ = 108

Lead me, guide me, walk with me to - day,

My heart is ten - der, I long to live your way;

Lead me, guide me, walk with me to - day,

I seek your bless - ing up - on me as I pray.

My spir - it needs a gen - tle touch;

Op - en my heart to feel a com - fort - ing friend who

dwells with me, and makes the path so clear.

As   you   prom - ised   dis - ci - ples   long   a - go,
Hear   me,   heal   me,   speak   peace   un - to   my   soul,

You   sent   a   mess - en - ger   to   me —   the   Ho - ly   Ghost;
Teach   me,   and   guard   me,   to   your   gift   can make   me   whole;

Like   a   whis - per,   the   Spir - it's   voice   is   heard
Dear - est   Sav - ior,   I   long   to   see   your   face,

bring - ing   to   my   re - mem - brance   your   e - ter - nal   word.
ten - der   and   so   fa - mil - iar,   bright   and   full   of   grace.

My spir - it needs a gen - tle touch, bring - ing me to my knees;
My spir - it needs a gen - tle touch; Op - en my heart to hear a

Teach - ing me truths that have no end of com - fort and peace. All my life is in your hands,
com - fort - ing friend who dwells with me, and makes the path so clear.

the Spir - it whis - pers all that I should know; Now I give my mind and will to you,

I know your great - est gift can save my soul.
makes the path so clear.

GOOD
WORKS

Good Works

VALUE EXPERIENCE

Bigger and Better Scavenger Hunt

For a Young Women and Young Men activity: What could be more fun than a scavenger hunt? How about a scavenger hunt that gives you the opportunity to do a good work at the same time? This activity is called Bigger and Better because at every house each team attempts to add one item to their collection that is bigger and better than the item they were given at the previous home.

How to play: Divide into teams of one leader and four or five youth. Set travel parameters (ward members only) and a finish time. Each team is given one small straight pin. Teams dash off to the first house, show the little pin, and ask if the family would like to give them something "bigger and better" to donate to Deseret Industries or other charitable organization. That family may offer a very small item, such as an action-figure toy. The team then takes that small item to the next place and asks for something "bigger and better." This continues until there is nothing bigger to be found, or until the time runs out.

Awards: Teams meet back at the church to be judged for their collections:
First place—awarded to the team who has collected the "biggest" item
Second place—awarded to the team with the "best" object
Third place—awarded to the team that collects the largest total number of items

Follow up: Deliver all donated items to Deseret Industries or a local thrift store.

GOAL: Have fun working together for a good cause!

TIME: 60 minutes for the scavenger hunt
            Travel time to deliver donated items

SUPPLIES: Straight pin for each team
            Ward directory and map for each team
            Transportation for each team
            Bags or boxes

HINT: Teams may need to have pickup trucks to carry the collected items. The biggest donation could be a backyard barbeque grill or a queen-size mattress!

Good Works

Cookies and Caroling

Celebrate the Savior's gift to you, by giving gifts to others. Make treats for neighbors, and deliver them with a song!

With your family: Prepare a traditional family recipe, such as your great-grandmother's spice cake. Arrange the treat on a covered plate, adding a greeting tag from your family. Ring the doorbell at your neighbor's house, and sing a Christmas carol. Keep singing as they come to the door; this lets your neighbors feel the spirit of Christmas with you. Give them the treat, mentioning that the recipe is famous in your family. Everyone will feel a joyful spirit.

For a Young Women activity: We love to cook! Prepare a special treat together, or ask each young woman to bring something she has baked at home. Deliver these to selected neighbors, along with beautiful Christmas carols sung especially for them.

GOAL: Share your Christmas joy with your neighbors.

TIME: 30–60 minutes to prepare treats
10 minutes to deliver them with a song

SUPPLIES: As listed in recipe
Gift tag to color (see below)

HINT: Choose a backup neighbor, in case someone is not at home.

Good Works

VALUE EXPERIENCE
Sing a Song of Service

How can you walk in the Savior's footsteps? As you share your gifts and your love with others, you are emulating Jesus Christ's work on the earth.

On your own: Study and learn the lyrics of the song "If You Love Me" on pages 112–115 of this book. Ask someone to play the music as you sing the words.

With your family: Learn and sing this song for a special family home evening. Make a family commitment to act as disciples of Christ in two ways for the next three weeks:

- Show kindness to everyone with whom you interact. For example, be patient at slow checkout lines, allow drivers to merge in front of you, or go out of your way to talk to someone who seems alone.

- Seek opportunities to share the gospel. For example, invite neighbors to participate in a service activity your ward is sponsoring, or mention in conversation your family's recent trip to the temple.

As a Young Women's group: Learn and sing "If You Love Me" as a choir in Young Women meetings.

GOAL: Make a personal commitment to act as a disciple of Christ to all you meet.

TIME: 30–60 minutes to learn and sing the song several times.

HANDOUTS: Music for the song "If You Love Me" on pages 112–115

SUPPLIES: Copies of the music
            Singers
            Piano and pianist

HINT: Do you love to perform? Ask Young Women leaders to help schedule a date to sing this song as a Young Women's group for Young Women in Excellence or another special event.

PROJECT: You can expand this activity into a Value Project by leading a Young Women choir as they prepare and perform this song:

GOOD WORKS VALUE PROJECT
Teach a Song: "If You Love Me," p. 110

Good Works

Child Care for Choir

Make the world safe for singers! Many young couples or single parents have difficulty participating in ward choir because of the potential disruptions caused by an infant or several young children. Offer your babysitting skills to enable the parents to praise the Lord in song.

On your own: Volunteer to care for young children during your ward's choir practice each week. Make arrangements with your bishop and the choir director to entertain a few young children in a separate area at the church or wherever the choir rehearses. Be sure to bring items that will capture and keep a small person's attention. Consider offering this service during preparations for Easter or Christmas musical programs, as many people will particularly want to be part of these holiday celebrations.

As a Young Women's group: Form a regular babysitting service during choir rehearsals. Depending on the number of children present, you may want two or three young women to serve each week. Write up a schedule and rotate the responsibility. Coordinate this effort with your bishop, the choir director, and your Young Women leaders.

GOAL: With a willing heart, offer a meaningful service to ward members.

TIME: 60 minutes each week

HANDOUT: Announcement on page 103

SUPPLIES: Toys and supplies appropriate for young children:
- Storybooks
- Puzzles
- Trucks
- Bubbles
- Crayons and paper

HINT: The ward nursery and toys are generally not available for children at this time. You will want to bring your own tried and true babysitting kit and other supplies.

PROJECT: Offer this service all year!

Childcare for Choir!

When: _____

Where: _____

Ages: _____

Service provided by:

_____

_____

Childcare for Choir!

When: _____

Where: _____

Ages: _____

Service provided by:

_____

_____

Good Works

VALUE EXPERIENCE
The Christmas Orange

This "sweet" story can become a tradition to share with those you love each Christmas holiday. The tale is an old-fashioned one, but the suffering, goodness, and generosity described in the story are timeless. As the scripture tells us, *"Inasmuch as ye have done it unto one of the least of these my brethren, ye have done it unto me" (Matthew 25:40).*

With your family: Present this story for family home evening. Gather in a circle and read the story to your family members. Wait a moment at the conclusion of the tale for everyone to understand exactly what happened. Then with great ceremony, open your one perfect orange, and invite each person to have a section. Savor the flavor of a gift given with love.

For a Young Women activity: Tell this story to a circle of young women, and then share the orange, section by section. You could give each girl a fresh orange with a copy of the story to take home to share with her family.

GOALS: Gain greater appreciation for friends and family as you contemplate the generosity of the children in this story.

            Seek out ways to express your own generous spirit throughout the coming year.

TIME: 15 minutes, not including shopping

HANDOUT: "The Christmas Orange" story on the following page

SUPPLIES: Copies of story
            Real orange for each participant *or* chocolate orange to share

HINT: Chocolate oranges will separate easily into 20 sections.

PROJECT: As you discuss those who are less fortunate than you, consider making a long-term service commitment:

                    GOOD WORKS VALUE PROJECT
                    Soup-Kitchen Commitment, p. 107

The Christmas Orange
By Fred C. LeMon (1920–73)

However impossible and elusive the Christmas message may seem some years, I always take a great comfort in the story of a little orphan boy, whom we shall refer to as "Jake" for want of more variety in the matter.

Jake was a resident of an orphan's home, one of ten children supported by what contributions the home could secure on a continuous struggle. There was very little to eat. It was seldom very warm in the wintertime, for fuel was expensive. But at Christmastime there always seemed to be a little more to eat and the home seemed a little warmer; it was a time for more than the usual enjoyment. But more than this, there was an orange. This was the only time of the year that such a rare item was provided— and it was coveted by each child like no other thing they ever possessed. They would save it for several days. Admiring it, feeling it, loving it, and contemplating the moment when they would eat it. Truly it was the "piece de resistance" to the Christmastide, and the year, for many would wait until New Year's Day or later to eat it. Oftentimes it would start to dry out and shrivel before they would eat it in order to salvage what they could.

This Christmas Day Jake had offended the rules or authority of the home in some manner and his punishment was loss of the orange privilege. After a year of waiting for this rare occasion, and this most desired of all rewards, it was denied. Plaintiff pleading was to no avail. Although the offence was rather minor, still it was an infraction of rules that must govern in regulated society. Jake spent Christmas Day empty and alone—it even seemed the other children didn't want to associate with a person who didn't have an orange.

Nighttime arrived and this was worst of all. Jake could not sleep. There was no love in the world. There was no forgiving. And certainly there could be no God that would permit a contrite little soul to suffer so much by himself. Silently he sobbed for the future of mankind and the world perhaps; but mostly because he didn't have an orange like the other kids had.

A soft hand placed on Jake's shoulders startled him momentarily and an object was quickly shoved into his hands. The donor disappeared into the dark of the room, leaving Jake with what he did not immediately identify as an orange. Not a regular run-of-the-orchard, but one fabricated from segments of nine other oranges. Nine other highly prized oranges that would of necessity be eaten this day instead of several days hence.

MAY THE GOOD LORD BLESS AND PROSPER YOU
THIS DAY AND ALWAYS!

Good Works

VALUE EXPERIENCE

Secret Sister

On your own: Prayerfully choose one person who is in need of special attention. Secretly do many kind acts of service for that person for one month. You may choose your actual sister or a "sister" in your young women's group or anyone else you feel can benefit from your special kindness.

With your family: Ask each family member, including your parents, to write his or her name on a slip of paper and drop it into a hat. Invite everyone to draw out one name from the hat. (Choose again if you get your own name.) Without revealing whose name you picked, do many acts of kindness and service for this family member for the next two weeks. Keep your actions secret! For example, your sister's bed may magically make itself every day while she is in the shower! At family home evening two weeks later, ask each family member to try to guess who their secret sister (or brother) has been! Have you made a difference in someone's life?

As a Young Women's group: Draw names among one class or among the entire group of young women in your ward. For one month, you will be the "secret sister" to the person whose name you drew. Each girl promises to secretly do something to show her love for her "sister" at least once a week during this time, and commits to look out for her at every opportunity. Set a $3 *total* spending limit to encourage creativity and a personal touch. Each young woman should carefully plan many ways to serve her sister for this special month. For example, she could sit beside her "sister" during Sunday School class, offer a compliment when she looks especially nice, find out her favorite candy bar and have it mysteriously delivered to her home, or invite her to join a group of friends during lunch at school.

GOAL: Practice selflessness as you perform secret acts of kindness for someone else.

TIME: Approximately 1 hour

SUPPLIES: Open heart and willing hands

HINT: At the end of the "secret sister" time period, you may want to choose a *new* person and simply continue being kind!

Good Works

VALUE PROJECT
Soup-Kitchen Commitment

"For I was an hungred, and ye gave me meat: I was thirsty, and ye gave me drink. . . . Inasmuch as ye have done it unto one of the least of these my brethren, ye have done it unto me" (Matthew 25:35–40).

On your own, with your family, or for a YW/YM activity: Gain real satisfaction as you give your time and your heart serving those who are less fortunate. Contact a local soup kitchen and commit to regular service at their facility. Then open your heart as you spend time with some of Heavenly Father's children.

How to start: If you have no idea how to start, first telephone your county or city government services. They can refer you to agencies and homeless shelters in your area. You may also contact Catholic Services; they are leaders in offering community assistance to those in need. Many food service organizations specialize in family dining. It can be especially rewarding to assist in feeding small children and mothers.

Lending your hand: Your service may be exactly that: serving plates of food to those in need. You may also be involved in food preparation. Many food banks prepare thousands of meals for delivery each week. You may be asked to make 200 sandwiches, or load a list of items into boxes for families. Look at each person you serve as an individual, a beloved child of God. Smile as you make eye contact; start a friendly conversation. The person may not always speak English, but you can still communicate that you care.

GOALS: Make a difference in the lives of families and individuals who are living in poverty. Serve with willing hands and a warm heart.

As you mingle with people who are in difficult circumstances, become more aware of how Heavenly Father's love extends to all of His children.

TIME: 10+ hours

HINT: Be aware that soup kitchens are logically located; this means they are in areas of town that could be unsafe. Do not expose yourself to danger; instead, go with a group or with adults, and preferably in the daytime.

VALUE EXPERIENCE: This short activity may inspire you to serve:
GOOD WORKS VALUE EXPERIENCE: The Christmas Orange, p. 104

Good Works

VALUE PROJECT

Food Collection and Contest

Develop your leadership abilities as you organize a substantial food drive. Publicize the food drive with flyers and announcements in the ward bulletin. Include a list of suggested items and the date and time of the food collection.

To prepare for this activity, consult with a local food bank. The director of the organization will recommend food items that are most useful to those in need, and may also provide large plastic barrels to collect donations.

For a Young Women and Young Men activity: Enlisting the aid of youth in your ward gives them an opportunity to serve others! Collect canned goods and other nonperishable food items. All food donated will be given to an organization that specializes in delivering food to those in need.

Contest: To make this activity a lot of fun, teams will compete to gather the largest total number and the most unusual item of food! Award prizes!

GOALS: Gather food items for those in need.

Learn gratitude for the blessings you have and appreciation for the generosity of others.

TIME: 10+ hours, including time to
- Make arrangements with the food bank
- Pick up collector barrels or boxes
- Prepare and distribute announcements
- Plan other publicity (ward bulletin announcement, etc).
- Lead youth in gathering food donations
- Load food in barrels or boxes and into truck
- Deliver food to local organization, and unload

HANDOUT: Announcement on page 109

SUPPLIES: Announcements
Small boxes or bags for each team
Boxes or barrels

HINT: Don't load too much into each box; you will have to lift it later!

VALUE EXPERIENCE: Participate in a food collection for Good Works.

Food Collection
& Contest!

Date: _____
Time: _____
Place: _____

Donations will benefit: _____

Food Collection
& Contest!

Date: _____
Time: _____
Place: _____

Donations will benefit: _____

Good Works

VALUE PROJECT

Teach a Song:
"If You Love Me"

With approval from your Young Women leaders, learn and then help teach the song "If You Love Me" to a group of young women. Arrange an opportunity for them to perform as a choir.

LEARN: Study and learn the lyrics of "If You Love Me" on pages 112–115 of this book. Play, or invite someone to play the music, as you sing the words.

TEACH: After you are familiar with the song, you can help teach it to the young women of your ward. Notice that everyone sings the melody together most of the time. There is a higher harmony part that will add fullness and beauty to the song. Ask a few sopranos to learn and sing this part while the rest of the choir sings the lower notes.

PERFORM: Choose a performance date about six weeks ahead, to allow time to polish all parts. Lead the Young Women's group as they sing "If You Love Me" for your ward's sacrament meeting or other special occasion.

GOALS: Remember that the Savior's life was filled with service to others; commit to be His disciple and follow in His footsteps.

Increase leadership skills as you make arrangements, teach, and lead rehearsals and performances.

Follow through with your commitment, even if others are not always dependable.

TIME: 10+ hours, including time to
  • Study the lyrics and understand the message of the song
  • Sing and play through the song several times
  • Arrange with leaders for dates to teach it to young women
  • Copy and organize the sheet music
  • Learn how to teach and direct music
  • Notify and remind choir members of practice times
  • Arrange performance date
  • Plan, set up space, and lead musical rehearsals
  • Warm up and perform

Teach a Song:
"If You Love Me"
(CONTINUED)

HANDOUTS: Music for the song "If You Love Me" on pages 112–115

SUPPLIES: Copies of the sheet music for all young women choir members
Music folders (optional but gives an elegant look as you perform)
Accomplished musician, to be your "assistant"
Singers in two groups
Piano and pianist
Calendar to check dates
Treats (optional but rewarding at the end of song practice)

HINTS: Ask all choir members to be especially Christlike as they work together to learn and perform this song. The Spirit of the Lord will truly be felt as you sing.

To include all your ward's young women in your choir, ask your Young Women leaders if they will allow you to teach and to practice the music during opening exercises on Sundays. Be sure to schedule in advance which Sundays you may rehearse. Be careful to stick to the time limit they give you.

VALUE EXPERIENCE:
Young women may accomplish this goal as they sing:

GOOD WORKS VALUE EXPERIENCE
Sing a Song of Service, p. 101

If You Love Me

Words & Music by
Jeanni Hepworth Gould

With commitment, ♩ = 100

1. In my heart I feel a deep de - sire to serve the
2. There is some - thing in my soul, a can - dle burn - ing

Lord; I pon - der in my mind how best to
bright; I re - cog - nize I car - ry to the

act up - on His word. Re - mem - ber His com - pas - sion as He
Lord's e - ter - nal light. I can - not heal a blind man's eyes, but

John 8:7-12, 21:17

113

His com - mis - sion I will keep.

3. When

 ff

ff

molto rit.

Je - sus heard the judg - ments of the world, He spoke this

mp

a tempo

mp

word: Let he who has no sin be first to

cast a stone at her. The wo - man gained for -

mf

giveness; May I be the first to stand, and reach

out to-ward my bro-ther a lov-ing, ten-der

hand. I prom-ise I will love my neigh-bor,

as I love the Lord.

INTEGRITY

Integrity

On Time All the Time

Get your watch ready! Accomplishing this goal will have you checking the time often. You may even find you have time to spare! Commit yourself, for three weeks, to be on time for everything: from school to soccer to supper. Your busy schedule should give you lots of opportunity to work on punctuality as you complete this goal.

How to: Start your day off on the right foot as you arise with your alarm's first ring. Catch your ride to school with no delay. Be in your seat before the bell for every class. Make it to the practice field exactly at the scheduled start time. Be on time for your trumpet lesson. Get a comfortable bench in the chapel for church on Sunday instead of sitting on the folding chairs in the overflow.

Reaching your goal: Enjoy the peaceful feeling of not rushing from place to place. Arriving on time—or even a little early—will give you a few moments to relax and mentally prepare for each activity. An added benefit of your choice to always be on time is the reputation you will gain for being dependable.

With your family: Enlist the cooperation of your parents, siblings, or friends who will provide transportation for you to various activities and locations. As they recognize the worthiness of your goal, they will try hard to honor your request for punctuality.

GOALS: Show respect for yourself and others by being on time for everything for three weeks.

Earn a reputation for being a reliable person who keeps her word.

TIME: Absolutely none! In fact you will *gain* time from this experience.

SUPPLIES: Alarm clock
Watch
Reliable transportation

HINT: Try to be patient with those not yet enlightened about time commitments. Remember, you were once the same! As you wait for your teammates or others to arrive, have something ready to usefully occupy your time. For example, get a head start on your homework so you'll have more free time at home!

Integrity

VALUE EXPERIENCE

Thank Heaven for Little Girls!

For a Young Women activity: Your Young Women group will giggle in delight as you pretend to be "little girls" for one evening! A leader may secretly get baby pictures of each girl, and arrange them onto a poster. As you arrive for the activity, admire how adorable each baby is, and then try to match the photo with each young woman now.

Sharing time: Invite each young woman to bring a favorite storybook and special "friend" to the activity. Every young woman takes a turn to share a memory of her special doll or stuffed animal and then passes it around for hugs. Then each girl, with her most animated voice, reads aloud from her storybook. Discuss the sweet innocence of children, and read together the scripture Matthew 18:4. Accept the challenge to be not childish, but childlike.

Wind up the evening (and the young women!) with a rousing game of Duck, Duck, Goose! Serve pink-frosted animal cookies and milk for a delicious treat.

GOALS: Be loving, like a little child.

             Recommit to being honest in all your dealings.

             Remember that baptism and repentance can make us clean and
             pure like a little child again.

TIME: 60–90 minutes (perfect for a Young Women midweek activity)

HANDOUT: Invitation on page 119

SUPPLIES: Invitations
             Photograph of each young woman as a baby
             Poster board and rubber cement to mount photos
             Animal cookies with pink icing
             Milk
             Napkins and Dixie cups

             Each girl should bring:
             Favorite stuffed animal or doll
             Favorite storybook

118

Thank Heaven For Little Girls!

Date: _____

Time: _____

Place: _____

*Bring a doll or stuffed animal and
your favorite storybook to share!*

Thank Heaven For Little Girls!

Date: _____

Time: _____

Place: _____

*Bring a doll or stuffed animal and
your favorite storybook to share!*

Integrity

VALUE EXPERIENCE

Quote-a-Week

"You never stand alone when you stand with God and his prophets. Crowds had a great time laughing and pointing at Noah, but in the end it wasn't Noah who missed the boat."
   Brad Wilcox, *Growing Up: Gospel Answers About Maturation and Sex, 2000.*

Collect and prepare a book of 52 uplifting quotations, one for each week of the year. Learn from the wise words of prophets, parents, and philosophers. Write each quotation on a page of card stock, decorate as desired, punch two holes at the top of each page, and then thread through two large rings to form a book. Read the quotation daily, changing to a new quotation each week. As you read the wise words, you will learn from the counsel they offer, renew your commitment to choose the right, and be inspired to improve every day.

With your family: Share your wise and witty sayings with your family and friends. Display the book in an area of your home where everyone can be encouraged by the inspiring message you have chosen. You should know: *"If you don't stand for something, you'll fall for anything." Unknown*

GOALS: Commit to stand for righteous values as you search out and study messages of wisdom and truth.

Compile worthy quotations into a book to display and share.

TIME: 1–3 hours

HANDOUT: "Quick Quotations" to get you started on page 121

SUPPLIES: Church magazines and other sources of quotations
            Card stock (may be cut in half to create a smaller book)
            Pens or markers
            Handheld paper punch
            2 large rings

HINT: Make a book of 26 pages, and write quotations on both sides.

PROJECT: Gather worthy quotations as you complete this Value Project:

INTEGRITY VALUE PROJECT
Listen to a Prophet's Voice, p. 127

Quick Quotations

"If you believe you can do something, you're right." Vickey Pahnke *(February 2000)*

"To realize the value of ONE YEAR, ask a student who failed a grade.
To realize the value of ONE MONTH, ask a mother who gave birth to a premature baby.
To realize the value of ONE WEEK, ask the editor of a newspaper.
To realize the value of ONE HOUR, ask the lovers who are waiting to meet.
To realize the value of ONE MINUTE, ask a person who missed the train.
To realize the value of ONE SECOND, ask a person who just avoided an accident.
To realize the value of ONE MILLISECOND, ask the person who won a silver medal in the Olympics. Today is a gift. That's why it's called the present!" Unknown

"You are good. But it is not enough just to be good. You must be good for something." Gordon B. Hinckley *(October 2000)*

"If ignorance is bliss, why aren't more people happy?" Unknown

"Angels can fly because they take themselves lightly." Unknown

"The Lord works from the inside out. The world works from the outside in." Ezra Taft Benson *(November 1985)*

"Anger always drives the mouth faster than the mind." Unknown

"A closed mouth gathers no foot." Unknown

"A truly happy person is one who can enjoy the scenery on a detour." Unknown

"When obedience ceases to be an irritant and becomes our quest, in that moment God will endow us with power." Ezra Taft Benson *(1988)*

"Pessimist: One who complains about the noise when opportunity knocks." Unknown

"Federal law: Ten thousand books explaining the Ten Commandments." Unknown

"What part of 'Thou shalt not . . .' didn't you understand?" God
"Have you read my #1 best seller? There will be a test!" God *(Smith Advertising, 1998)*

"Holding a grudge is like drinking poison, and then waiting for the other person to die." Unknown

"Anger is a wind that blows out the lamp of reason." Unknown

"We could learn a lot from crayons: some are sharp, some are pretty, some are dull, some have weird names, and all are different colors . . . but they all have to learn to live in the same box." Unknown

"Never put both feet in your mouth at the same time, because then you don't have a leg to stand on." Unknown

"If you feel far away from God, who moved?" Unknown

"Our lives are, in reality, the sum total of our seemingly unimportant decisions and of our capacity to live by those decisions." Gordon B. Hinckley *(August 2000)*

Integrity

VALUE EXPERIENCE

Beautiful Values

On your own or for a Young Women activity: Create a lasting work of art that will always remind you to live the seven Young Women values.

How to press flowers: Gather fresh petite flowers from your garden. Carefully arrange tiny petals and leaves, and lay them flat between sheets of wax paper or commercial flower-press liners. Press firmly between pages of hardback books or in a flower press. Allow flowers to dry for several weeks, and then gently lift off the paper. Be sure to dry extra flowers, as they are very fragile to work with.

Art design: Copy the Beautiful Values special background paper (see page 123) onto high-quality linen paper. Using tweezers, arrange pressed flowers along the oval that encircles the Young Women values. Your flowers will form a beautiful border to frame the words. When you have a design that is visually pleasing, gently glue the flowers in place. Enhance your finished artwork with a colored mat board, trim paper to 8"x10", cover it with glass, and then place it carefully in a frame. You will be pleased to display your Beautiful Values as a reflection of your beauty within.

GOALS: Remind yourself of the importance of the Young Women values, and strive to incorporate them into your life on a daily basis.

Create a lovely display to decorate your home.

TIME: 30 minutes to select and press flowers to dry
3 weeks to wait for them to dry
30 minutes to arrange into a beautiful display

HANDOUT: Beautiful Values background paper on page 123

SUPPLIES: Beautiful Values background paper, copied onto high-quality paper
Small flowers of several types
Spanish moss or other delicate dried fern leaves
Glue
Colored 8"x10" mat board, with 5"x7" opening for picture
Frame with glass, 8"x10"

HINT: Experiment with your design! You may choose to place flowers at the top and bottom of the oval and then simply add tiny stems of Spanish moss or greenery along the curved sides.

Faith

Divine Nature

Individual Worth

Knowledge

Choice and Accountability

Good Works

Integrity

(Mat board will cover this area.)

Integrity

Speak in Sacrament Meeting

Willingly accept the call to speak in your ward's sacrament meeting. Your cheerful agreement may surprise your bishop—and also make his day!

Prepare: Prayerfully contemplate the topic you were given. Seek out helpful resources such as the *New Era* and *Ensign* magazines, the Church web site at www.lds.org, gospel books, and most especially, the standard works. Read extensively on your topic, and then determine your main focus. Start with an outline of the points you wish to communicate. Add supporting scriptures and quotes from Church leaders. (See talk outline on the following page.)

Present: Speak slowly and clearly—the natural tendency when nervous is to talk far too fast. Become so familiar with your message that you can make eye contact with your listeners. Let your personality and the joy you have in the gospel shine through. Finally, connect with your listeners by sharing a personal experience on the subject; as Nephi taught, liken the scriptures unto yourself.

With your family: Invite your parents to listen as you practice your talk in advance. They can offer encouragement and a few helpful suggestions.

GOALS: Increase the depth and breadth of your knowledge on a particular gospel topic.

Share your understanding and your testimony of this principle with others in your ward.

TIME: 2 or more hours to prepare
Less than 10 minutes to present

HANDOUT: Talk outline on page 125

SUPPLIES: Talk outline
Scriptures
Church books and magazines
Church web site (optional)

HINT: Remember, when you give a talk or a lesson,
you are the one who learns the most!

Don't be timid— just be yourself!

Speak in Sacrament Meeting

TOPIC: _____ DATE: _____

Don't be timid— just be yourself!

Main Ideas:

1. _____
_____
_____
2. _____
_____
_____
3. _____
_____
_____

Add these to strengthen and support your message:

1. Scriptures:

2. Statements from the prophet:

3. Short excerpts from conference talks:

4. Short excerpts from *Ensign* or *New Era* magazines:

5. Personal experiences that relate to the theme:

6. Your personal testimony of this gospel principle:

Integrity

Sing a Sacred Song

This gentle and pure melody will play softly in your mind after you have learned it, reminding you of your promise to be worthy to enter the temple.

On your own: Study and learn the lyrics of the song "Sacred Promises" found on pages 132–135 of this book. Play, or ask someone to play the music, as you sing the words. Commit to be worthy at all times to enter the temple.

With your family: Learn and sing this song for a special family home evening. Ask your parents or older siblings to describe their feelings upon entering the temple for the first time to receive their endowments.

As a Young Women's group: Learn and sing "Sacred Promises" as a choir in Young Women meetings. There are three separate parts; each part is very easy to learn and sing. As you sing together, appreciate the pure sound of the harmony, and feel a sacred reverence for dressing in purest white and entering the temple.

GOALS: Prepare now to be temple worthy.

                 Be worthy to enter the temple to perform baptisms for the dead.

TIME: 30–60 minutes to learn and sing the song several times.

HANDOUTS: Music for the song "Sacred Promises" on pages 132–135

SUPPLIES: Copies of the music
              Singers divided into three groups
              Piano and pianist

HINT: Learn this song in preparation for attending the temple to perform baptisms for the dead.

BONUS: Ask Young Women leaders to help schedule a date to sing "Sacred Promises" as a Young Women's group for sacrament meeting.

PROJECT: You can expand this activity into a musical Value Project by leading a Young Women choir as they prepare and perform this song:

INTEGRITY VALUE PROJECT
Teach a Song: "Sacred Promises," p. 130

Integrity

VALUE PROJECT

Listen to a Prophet's Voice

It is a privilege to hear our beloved prophet and the Lord's chosen leaders speak directly to us. Pay special attention to the message each general conference speaker chooses to share. You are receiving modern-day revelation as you listen. Did you know that the speakers are not assigned topics? They each seek to follow the inspiration of the Spirit as they select and prepare their talks.

On your own or with your family: Participate completely in a general conference of The Church of Jesus Christ of Latter-day Saints. Attend and listen closely to the satellite broadcast from the Young Women general presidency on the Saturday before a spring general conference weekend. Watch and listen attentively to all four sessions of general conference on the scheduled Saturday and Sunday. As you listen, refer to a chart and photos of the general authorities. You can find this in the exact center of the *Ensign's* conference reports (May or November issue).

Journal: Take notes of the wise counsel directed to you. Write about your feelings as you receive this counsel with an open heart.

GOALS: Receive with an open heart the messages of our prophet and other Church leaders.

Recognize the importance of attentively listening to the revealed counsel from the Lord for our day.

TIME: 90 minutes for Young Women broadcast
4 hours for Saturday sessions
4 hours for Sunday sessions
30 minutes to write in your journal

SUPPLIES: Location to hear satellite broadcasts
Television station that receives general conference (if possible)
General authority chart, from *Ensign*
Journal and pen

HINT: General conference is nearly always the weekend of the first Sunday in April, and the weekend of the first Sunday in October.

Integrity

You Should Be Committed!

You have made a commitment to read the entire Book or Mormon or to be captain of the colorguard or to maintain a clean and tidy bedroom—or to do something else that is a difficult and ongoing challenge. But after a while, you find yourself struggling to stay awake to read, or holding the bag when others are quitting the team, or knocking over a trash can with frustration, or otherwise losing the motivation to succeed.

Just at the moment you are ready to give up, along comes this project! Make a promise to yourself to completely fulfill your goal. Commit to conquer all obstacles in your path with your dedication to succeed. Fill in and sign the Complete Commitment Form on the following page.

GOALS: When you are very tempted to throw in the towel, stick with and accomplish a substantial goal you have set for yourself.

Be responsible and honest with yourself and others.

"If at first you don't succeed, try, try again!"

TIME: 10+ hours

HANDOUT: Complete Commitment Form on page 129

SUPPLIES: Complete Commitment Form
Journal
Pen
Kleenex (optional, for your tears)

HINT: After filling in and signing the Complete Commitment Form, hang it in a place where you will see it on a regular basis, such as on the bathroom mirror or the refrigerator door. Choose a place you cannot avoid!

PROJECT: Can't find a difficult activity to commit to? Work on this challenging project at the same time:

FAITH VALUE PROJECT
Book of Mormon, p. 12

Complete Commitment Form

1. Goal I have committed to accomplish: _____
_____
_____

2. Specific tasks I must perform to complete this
project: _____
_____
_____
_____
_____

3. Time period I have set to achieve this goal: ___
_____

4. Ways this achievement will help me in other
areas of my life: _____
_____
_____

I am completely committed to accomplishing this
goal!

Signed _____Date_____

Integrity

VALUE PROJECT

Teach a Song: "Sacred Promises"

This music can play gently in your mind, reminding you of your personal commitment to be worthy to enter the holy temple of the Lord.

With approval from your Young Women leaders, learn and then help teach the new song "Sacred Promises" to a group of young women. Arrange an opportunity for them to perform as a choir.

LEARN: Study and learn the lyrics of the song "Sacred Promises" on pages 132–133 of this book. Invite someone to play the music as you sing the words. Notice that there are four separate parts. Each part has its own melody and is very easy to learn and sing. Each part is sung separately, and then two parts are combined and sung together. At the finale, three parts are sung at one time. I promise, it is actually very easy!

TEACH: After you are familiar with the song and the four easy melody parts, you can begin to teach it to others. You may want to ask a music professional in your ward to assist. At the first rehearsal, have everyone learn every part. At later practices divide into groups, including one group of girls who enjoy singing high. They will sing the high part on the last page of the song.

As you sing together, appreciate the pure sound of the harmony, and feel a deep reverence for dressing in purest white and entering the holy temple.

PERFORM: Choose a performance date about six weeks ahead, to allow time to polish all parts. Lead the Young Women's group as they sing "Sacred Promises" for your ward's sacrament meeting or other special occasion.

GOALS: Commit to be temple worthy.

Increase leadership skills as you make arrangements, teach, and lead rehearsals and performances.

Follow through with your commitment, even if others are not always dependable.

Teach a Song:
"Sacred Promises"
(CONTINUED)

TIME: 10+ hours, including time to
- Study the lyrics and understand the message of the song
- Sing and play through the song several times
- Arrange with leaders for dates to teach it to young women
- Copy and organize the sheet music
- Learn how to teach and direct music
- Notify and remind choir members of practice times
- Arrange performance date with ward music chairman
- Plan, set up space, and lead musical rehearsals
- Warm up and perform

HANDOUTS: Music for the song "Sacred Promises" on pages 132–135

SUPPLIES: Copies of the music for all young women choir members
Music folders (optional but gives an elegant look as you perform)
Person who is knowledgeable about music and willing to teach you
Singers divided into three groups
Piano and pianist
Calendar to check dates
Treats (optional but rewarding at the end of song practice)

HINTS: Learn this song in preparation for attending the temple to perform baptisms for the dead.

To include all your ward's young women in your choir, ask your Young Women leaders if they will allow you to teach and to practice the music during opening exercises on Sundays. Be sure to schedule in advance which Sundays you may rehearse. Be careful to stick to the time limit they give you.

VALUE EXPERIENCE:
Young Women singers can achieve this goal:

INTEGRITY VALUE EXPERIENCE
Sing a Sacred Song, p. 126

131

Sacred Promises

Words & Music by
Jeanni Hepworth Gould

Clear and white, re-flect-ed in the wa-ter, ris-ing bright a-mid the col-ored blos-soms;

Strong and sure, a wit-ness of His prom-ise, is the tem-ple of God.

Dressed in pur-est white, I shall en-ter that ho-ly door;

Dressed in pur - est white, I shall en - ter that ho - ly door;

All I am and all I ev - er hope to be I of - fer to the Lord;

I am pre - pared to pledge o - be - di - ence to all my Fa - ther may com - mand;

Sa - cred prom - is - es I will cov - e - nant with the Lord.

All I am and all I ev - er hope to be I of - fer to the Lord.

Re - ceive the sa - cred bless - ings of this ho - ly place where heav - en's close at hand.

Sa - cred prom - is - es I will keep for e - ter - ni - ty; Blessed with light that leads to ex - al - ta - tion

through the tem - ple, the house of God.

Perfect Projects CD-ROM!

Perfect Projects is also available on CD–ROM, which includes:

- 22 Value Projects

- 43 Value Experiences

- Graphics, handouts, charts, and invitations

- 26 Color graphics to print on your color printer

- Sheet music for 7 songs for young women

Look for these music recordings by Jeanni Gould

- *10 Terrific Programs for New Beginnings and Young Women in Excellence*—10 songs for young women (Music CD/CD-ROM)

- *Midweek Treasures for Young Women*—11 songs for young women (Music CD/CD-ROM)

- Coming soon...
    Celebrate! Songs of the Savior—
12 songs: SATB, male/female duets, and solos (Music CD)